THE GOSPEL OF
LIBERATION

THE GOSPEL OF

LIBERATION

Jürgen Moltmann

Translated by H. WAYNE PIPKIN

WORD BOOKS,
Publisher
Waco, Texas

TO MY FRIENDS
BLAIR AND DOUG MEEKS
AND MY GODSON
JOHN

CONTENTS

Preface

Many pastors today find preaching difficult, more a burden than a joy. They ask whether it still makes sense to speak of God and God only. Many Christians have difficulty in following sermons. From television, radio, advertising, and politics there are so many other voices pressing on their ear. They question what role the sermon they are listening to can actually play in their lives.

I know these questions. For five years I have been a pastor in a small congregation near Bremen and still preach regularly in congregational worship and in university worship services. I also hear sermons regularly and, in common with other men, though I am often disappointed I am often inspired. In the midst of trouble and disappointment sermons hold for me a promise and a constant new hope. They are an incomparable joy, where God's joy and man's liberation always comes as word, where man steps back and the event itself is audible.

This "event" of the sermon is the living person of the

liberator Jesus Christ. In him comes the joy of God to an otherwise often joyless world. Through him fall the chains which often make men sad and angry. The joy of speaking or hearing of him is greater than human laziness and stubbornness. It is greater than all the sorrow that exists over the weak and apathetic church or over other men. It must also be greater than all the accusations and protests against the Establishment in church and society. For joy is the first and last word of liberation.

The sermons and radio talks which make up this book come from the last six years and were given at the universities of Wuppertal, Bonn, and Tübingen, or were broadcast over German radio. They are as demanding as the matter under discussion requires and as the hearers warrant.

Sermons belong in a worship service and a living community. It is a hazardous enterprise to publish them so that they can be read without the event of the worship service and without the situation of the concrete community. It is even a greater risk to translate sermons into another language and to publish them in another culture. If, however, sermons point beyond themselves to the "truth which makes free," then they may be able to bear translation. I am thankful to Word Books for undertaking on this basis the risk of translating my sermons into English and publishing them in the United States.

With the publication of these sermons I would like to testify that my well-known "theology of hope" is a theology *for* the church and not against it. According to my conviction, scholarly theology has for its target the sermon just as every recognition of truth aims at a practice which will change false reality. A theology of hope has for its goal a practical liberation of men from the chains of sin, of law, and of anxiety; its desire is to provide concrete liberation from the demonic circle of oppression, of exploitation, and of evil death. Though not the only means, the sermon is one of the best for liberating the internally and externally oppressed man for faith, love, and hope.

Theology must be critical toward a sleeping church and a torpid tradition. It must battle the idolatry of anxiety which is ruining our churches. But its earnest critique of the church is a critique in the name of the crucified and resurrected Christ, and in the name of his smallest brother in our world. Its critique must therefore be a critique of hope for a better church, a believing and authentic Church of Christ. All other criticism is superficial and inconsequential.

As the publication of my sermons in the United States signifies, I have hope for the Church of Christ, in spite of all the disgraceful circumstances to be found in it. I have hope for a fearless and, in imitation of Christ, a persistent church because I believe the promises of God. That is also my hope for your country, which I love, because I suffer with you in your crises and tensions. The promises of God make man free for faith and give us all hope for a more human world. For it is this world on which the cross of Christ stood, and where his resurrection took place in splendor for us all.

September 1973   JÜRGEN MOLTMANN

1

God Is Different

"Seek the Lord while he may be found,
   call upon him while he is near;
let the wicked forsake his way,
   and the unrighteous man his thoughts;
let him return to the Lord, that he may have mercy on him,
   and to our God, for he will abundantly pardon.
For my thoughts are not your thoughts,
   neither are your ways my ways, says the Lord.
For as the heavens are higher than the earth,
   so are my ways higher than your ways
   and my thoughts than your thoughts.
For as the rain and the snow come down from heaven,
   and return not thither but water the earth,
making it bring forth and sprout,
   giving seed to the sower and bread to the eater,
so shall my word be that goes forth from my mouth;
   it shall not return to me empty,
but it shall accomplish that which I purpose,
   and prosper in the thing for which I sent it."

                                        Isaiah 55:6–11, RSV

Lord Jesus Christ, we await your coming as we await peace in this time of its outer and inner absence. We await your coming as we hunger for righteousness and suffer in the injustice between peoples and classes. We await your coming as we thirst for freedom, for we are conscious of the chains of guilt and oppression. Give hope once again to those who have lost you. Give love anew to those who only coldly interact with one another. Open our eyes that we may begin to see a glimpse of your joy in our lives. All this we ask of you.

"Where then is the old man who calls himself God? Why does he not speak? Answer! Why are you silent? Why? There is no answer! Is there no answer? Is there then no, no word???" cried Wolfgang Borchert after the war in his writing *Draussen vor der Tür* [Outside the Door].

If we hear him and listen for the answer again today, we too encounter silence. Is there no answer? Here is someone sitting in the house to which he has adapted himself so thoroughly he cannot leave any more. There is a man still traveling and who must always continue to travel the route where he has prospered. Here is a man who had faith and has lost it and does not know how to obtain it again. There is one who has betrayed a trust and does not know how to change. Is there no answer? One man has given up prayer. Another has ventured into cruel, daily godlessness. Still another has committed himself to and been tied down by others. Is there no answer?

"Seek the Lord as long as he may be found," demands the prophet and thereby says two things: whoever does not seek persistently also will find nothing. Many give up too early. Whoever does not question receives no answer. Nothing will be done for the man who does not knock loudly on the door.

But he also says something else: where nothing is to be

found, there we also have nothing to seek. If there is no answer, then the question is also to no purpose. If the house is uninhabited, then it is useless to knock. It is not only man's fault if he does not find God. Man has sought, questioned, cried, and suffered—but it is God's responsibility that no answer has come; for he concealed himself, withdrew, and was not there. Seek God so long as he is to be found, for there is a time in which he is not to be found and gives no further answer.

"Where are you, Other? You are still always there!" Wolfgang Borchert supposed when he found no answer. And that was where his misunderstanding began—all our misunderstandings. The misunderstanding of the general religious faith of God is that God is always there, eternal, unchanging; that he does not run here and there as we do when we are in a hurry; that he lives in heaven like a great king in his palace. If we do not find him and are not admitted into his presence, then it is our fault for not having sought him in the appropriate form for an audience. So say the religions, with their practices of piety.

For the prophets in Israel, however, God is quite different than this "Other." He is a living God who leaves us and seeks us. He—he himself—leads into hell and out again. Therefore, there is in fact a time in which God is not to be found and actually gives no answer. Therefore, seek God so long as he is to be found.

If he comes near to us, then it is time to seek him. If he is far, then we cannot seek him but must remain where we are. It lies in God himself as to whether or not he will let himself be found or let us go out empty-handed. It is not time to get up until morning comes. So it is with God, too. If he announces that he is coming near, then it is time to pay attention and to seek him, to set out and go to meet him. Then torpid relationships begin to dance, and everything to which we have become so committed that we thought we could not change, turns into a game of possibilities and transformations.

Was there a time in Israel when the Lord was not to be found, when a leaden heaven overwhelmed everything? Were the Israelites like Wolfgang Borchert, "waiting outside the door"? Like him, did they question, toil, and curse—and then receive no answer? The prophet himself lived publicly in such a time (Isa. 40:27, 49:14). That was the lamentation of the captive, the dispersed, the humiliated, and the abandoned from Israel in the Babylonian exile. Is God impotent? Yes, he really had not helped in the destruction of the northern kingdom. Does God sleep? Indeed, he had remained silent through the destruction of Jerusalem. Is this God of history and of a covenant with the people no right God? In fact, they lost the promised land. They lost the city. They lost their history and their freedom. They lost their name, as one does in captivity and in guilt. Where was God keeping himself?

We know the complaint of this people: "By the waters of Babylon we sat down and wept." We know their faith, which was nothing more than a single open wound. "Why do you hide your face?" (Ps. 44:24) "Why do you sleep?" (Ps. 44:23) "Why are you like a stranger?" (Jer. 44:8) "Why are you silent?" (Job 1:13) "Why? Why?"

This questioning faith is like a groping in the dark. We know nothing further. We cannot change it. We know that this darkness comes from God himself, and that these stripes are grounded in the absence of God. They do not lie in man. It lies in God, when we are brought thus into sorrow, into exile, into solitude, and into questions without answers. Israel knew that. "There comes a call from Seir in Edom: Watchman, how long still the night? The watchman speaks: Morning comes but it is still night. If you want to question, then come again another time" (Isa. 21:11–12).

Many people today are of the opinion that this is indeed the last word about our situation in our time, from Wolfgang

Borchert to all those to whom God is dead or has simply, without their having noted it, gotten lost.

But the lesson of Deutero-Isaiah, the salvation-prophet of the forsaken in Babylon, is different. Seek the Lord now that he is to be found. Call on him now so long as he is near. Hear the word of God in the time of God. And the time of God is the end time, the end of exile, the end of silence, the end of forsakenness. The oppressing and burdening silence breaks, and the watchman whom we have before us in Deutero-Isaiah speaks, announcing the time of God: The night comes to an end. Morning breaks. If you want to question, then come now.

That is also the hour of the gospel of the anointed of God, who has come in our flesh, in our questions, in our pain, until the last cry on the cross. That is the time of the Messiah. To be sure, night and exile lie before us. Silencing questions and disappointing expectations gnaw at us. But in the coming of the Crucified, God himself approaches. Where he is near, his kingdom comes, and where his kingdom comes near, there hope comes seeking God in queries and in passion. There the chains are set free. The godless can leave his way, and the evildoer his thoughts and hallucinations. We can return. We can begin anew. We can lift our heads out of the mire of self-depreciation. Why? Because freedom approaches wherever God comes. The world is no longer unchangeable but can be transformed. Man is no longer damned in all eternity. The door is opened. It makes sense, therefore, to knock on the still closed doors.

How did the prophet arrive at this idea, which still contradicted fully the long experience of the captives in Babylon?

The prophet, having heard a saying of God, has a vision. Where he got it and how he arrived at it we do not know. But while he announces it, he begins to act, and that is enough for us. To be sure, one swallow does not make a summer, we say. But there are these early signs, omens, and promises in which a new future of God and man and also of the world makes itself known. They are ambiguous, hidden. They are without great authority, but they provoke, they attract and challenge. And the great questions and investigations begin where one perceives the first faint questioning call-note of freedom.

The saying in which the coming God approaches is, first of all, a harsh contradiction: "For my thoughts are not your thoughts, neither are your ways my ways, says the Lord." We know that God is different. He is by no means the fulfillment of human thoughts and the heavenly guarantee of human ways. When the Israelites came into exile, they experienced pain. If our expectations are negated, if our prayers are not heard, if we are led where we do not want to go, we get the impression that this contradiction is, in fact, true. God is entirely different from the idols we make because we need them. We stand under a dark fate. The godless proceed into godlessness. The evildoer receives what his deeds are worth. That is the curse of the evil deed—that it must bear continuing evil. Thus we think that God is different, unattainable for dying beings.

The disturbing, incomprehensible, and actually entirely other in this contradiction of God, however, is that God, once again, *is* entirely other than we think; that he is different. Our thoughts are thoughts of judgment. We are forsaken. We are forgotten. We have no future, our anxiety tells us. The thoughts of God, however, are thoughts of giving and of joy. The meaning intended here, you think, is that history is at an end, passé, no more. Give in to your fate; there is nothing to be changed.

But the thoughts of God are not like our dark thoughts. Our ways under the law we keep are not his ways. We condemn ourselves, but he does not condemn us. We are resigned to our fate, but he is not. We judge ourselves and others according to the iron law of reciprocity; but his is a law of "much forgiveness." Therein God *is*—no, actually *becomes*—different. He becomes converted; converted for men, he decides in favor of love, he forgives without basis, he rejoices in us and with us. To experience the differentness of God as judge over our wishes is difficult, but thus it is. We must put ourselves in that position. To catch hold of the differentness of God, however, in his unconditional accepting love, in his fully forgiving nearness, in his joy in people, is much more difficult. For that brings us to him no matter what the distance. He comes nearer to us than we are to ourselves.

Out of this contradiction—of the joy of God as over against the self-judgment of man—springs then the vision of a new creation of God through the effecting, creating word of his deed. Rain and snow fall on the parched land and make the desert fruitful. The thirsty find water and the hungry find nourishment. A new creation comes. Just as the first creation called into life from chaos a world where man can live; just as it banned the denying negation and called a living beauty into existence, so into this old, destroyed world, by the effecting word, a new creation is coming. And this word shall come, it is first announced here. It will be an effective, creating word. It will not return empty, but will do what pleases God. It will succeed where it is sent.

"In the beginning was the Word," says John. Here, however, it is reversed: at the end comes the word, and it brings with it the end of the worthless and godless forsakenness of the world.

Naturally, we have difficulty understanding what this "Word" can mean. What are words? For us they are empty symbols, signs, and smoke. We live in a society where we can use many words and say everything, but where words accomplish nothing more. That is the sorrow of the intellectual and also of the preacher. Our prophet also does not assert that his own word is this creative word of God. His own word announces first the coming of that word. He is a forerunner of this word. He prepares the way for this word so that we want to know about it, we wait on it, and seek it. It is the last word. And wherever we wait on this word, we know that the individual words are preparatory and penultimate words; the good words just as much as the evil; the proud, justifying words, and also the hard, judging words. "Last words"—how often we use them in order to put others down: "You are always this way!" "That's the way they are—the others." What presumption lies in these our last words after which there can only be "silence." But these last words and also the deadly silence pass away for whomever waits on the word of God. He comes in questions, placing the firmness and the skills of our judgments and affairs in question. He is no longer contented with ultimate answers. For the time of questioning is the time of hope, and the presupposition for questioning is the changeability of man and his relationships in the appearance of the coming new creation of all things.

What, however, is promised by the word that the prophet announces? "It shall not return empty, but it shall succeed where I send it." Empty-returning words we know well enough. They are words spoken in the wind and in the mist. They come back to us empty, without echo. But there are also succeeding words which bring about something new. Jesus took them as parables out of daily life (Luke 11:11 ff.). Where is there a father who, when asked by his child for bread, would give him a stone instead? Even though we are not entirely good men, we do not allow all the words directed to us to be empty. Even though we are hard, we can still give children good gifts. And there are other words which are heard. Parents hear the requests of their children and often fulfill them. A woman hears her lover. And we often hear the cry of the hungry in Biafra and South America and other war-torn and disaster-stricken countries. However, there are more unheard cries and requests in the world than there are ears to hear them or hands to fulfill them. That's one thing: succeeding words are words which are heard.

The productive word with which God creates what he wants is another thing. The dead no longer hear. Those who are brought to silence hear no one. What is nothing, what is no longer, has no ears. But that word whose coming the prophet announces over all hearers and listeners is still going. It is the word of a new creation out of nothing. Whoever waits on it seeks after "the God who gives life to the dead and calls into existence the things that do not exist" (Rom. 4:17). Certainly that is more than one can expect of human faith. But is there not a hope which can look the battlefields of history in the eye without despairing?

Faith in God who creates new life out of nothing is a faith that transforms death and life. It bears in itself the simple hope that the dead and the destroyed are not dead in any final sense, that those who have died have not passed away finally, but that justice will be done to them. And the Word in which the creative God comes grasps also that emptiness in which we are dying and brings the lost out again. Otherwise, God would not be God. His word loves to succeed and not fail. Those who wait on his word give nothing up for lost, where he himself gives up and writes off no one who abandons himself. What, finally, does this hope mean other than always to affirm: yes, yes, it shall succeed! Whoever trusts in the final success of the creating and saving word of God cannot give up anything or write off anyone, even though all experience hits him in the face. He begins to love.

According to the saying of God which the prophet announces to the men in exile, he then comes again himself to speak with a noble vision. The captives return home to the land of freedom. Joy abounds and peace accompanies them. The mountains through which they move begin to laugh. The trees on the border of their path clap their hands in joy. All nature applauds the experience. The hedges dry up and in their place grow firs which give shade. Thorns become stunted; in their place grow fragrant myrtles. Silent nature awakens and joins in the song of freedom. The exodus from captivity into freedom is no event of grim battle, but of contagious joy which the whole creation echoes. She begins to dance, to play, and to shout in exultation, as if she were herself free from a hateful spell which lay upon her.

Is that only poetry? I do not believe so. To me it appears rather that here the cosmic dimension of men's liberation has been paraphrased in images. Thus, according to Paul, the entire waiting creation yearns for the revelation of the children of God. "Because the creation itself will be set free from its bondage to decay and obtain the glorious liberty of the children of God," he says in Romans 8:21. In his own body man stands outside nature; but he is at the same time not only against it, he is also always a part of this world. His inhumanity affects this world just as his humanity has its effect. Indeed, he represents creation in himself. Where he is free, then creation is also free. On the other hand, if everything is not redeemed from the bond of alienation, then he also is not redeemed. There is no redemption of the soul without a liberation of the body. There will be no exodus out of the night of God's obscurity for man without a new habitable creation coming out of this world of chaos. Certainly the passage into freedom begins with man. With that small event at the time of the return from Babylonian exile it is presaged and first brought before the eye. It begins with the exodus of the faithful out of the internal and external captivity of this world. It begins with Jesus and the disciples, runs through history, and is before us now. But there is an all-encompassing passage into freedom. Nothing and no one is shut out from that.

Certainly that is a great thought. A little too great, perhaps, for our style. But the people perish if there is no longer any vision. Whoever thinks in general of God and seeks him is not permitted to think small of him.

Our question, however, is what shall I begin? Where shall I begin? We come then back to the beginning. Three things were named to us there in order to begin the passage into freedom.

1. Seek the Lord and call on him. According to everything which the prophetic text says to us, we are to pray from the heart and to question with the mind. The passage into freedom begins with calling, praying, and questioning after God. Today many are critical of prayer because they see it as an impotent wish in need. Help yourself, and God helps you—they think this would be better. But here prayer is the echo of God who comes near and the first step into freedom out of the godless chains of captivity. Whoever prays in this way, as the prophet intended, gains a foretaste of freedom where he is, and becomes free himself. He arises and seeks the Lord because he has heard the rumor that God is to be found. He no longer surrenders himself to his situation. He no longer submits to the jailer. He calls on the Lord since the Lord has called him. If we see that, then, hopefully, it becomes clear that prayer is not there only for children and despondent souls, but is the privilege of the free. Whoever prays and questions and seeks after God becomes free. He is permitted to become different. It is not degradation but a great freedom to pray. For in prayer we participate in the freedom of God; in the intercession we grasp the passage into freedom of the whole creation and thus transform ourselves.

2. The godless should leave his way. Certainly, in loneliness, where everyone is established in his way, that is not possible. However, in God's approach come new possibilities. One must not any longer as a godless one be godless. One can actually leave the haughtiness and bitterness against God and join in the joy of God. One sees the world differently from before. One sees through the horizon of the individual boundaries into the future. One sees the man next to him with different eyes, with the eyes of the joy of God.

3. The evildoer must return to the Lord. If he only stares

at the fate of his deeds, then he can actually not return, of course, but must continue further. But if God comes with his forgiveness, then the evildoer can change himself and return. Grasped by the joy in God, he is no longer tied to his crimes, but free because he is loved.

How does freedom thus begin? It begins with prayer, with the permission to be different, and with the way into the joy of God. Where does it end? It ends in the new creation of all things and relationships.

God comes. Let us break open everything toward him and break off everything that will hinder us.

Out of the depths we cry, Lord, to you. Lord, hear our voices and lead us into freedom. Out of the depths the dead in Viet Nam cry to you, and also those who have killed them. Lord, hear their voices and swallow death with the victory of life. Out of the depths cry to you the hungry in Africa, Asia, and South America; and also the satiated in Europe who let them hunger. Lord, hear their voices and return us to justice.

Out of the depths cry to you the degraded and silenced in tyranny and also the great and small tyrants. Lord, hear their voices and destroy their anxiety and their haughtiness.

Out of the depths cry to you those "waiting outside the door," and those to whom no one can give a good answer. Lord, hear their voices and open your joy to your creation and your boundless love.

We wait on your word.
We hope for your kingdom.
We inquire after your truth.
We trust you for the sake of Jesus.

2

The God of Hope

For whatever was written in former days was written for our instruction, that by steadfastness and by the encouragement of the scriptures we might have hope. May the God of steadfastness and encouragement grant you to live in such harmony with one another, in accord with Christ Jesus, that together you may with one voice glorify the God and Father of our Lord Jesus Christ.

Welcome one another, therefore, as Christ has welcomed you, for the glory of God. For I tell you that Christ became a servant to the circumcised to show God's truthfulness, in order to confirm the promises given to the patriarchs, and in order that the Gentiles might glorify God for his mercy. As it is written,
"Therefore I will praise thee among the Gentiles,
  and sing to thy name";
and again it is said,
"Rejoice, O Gentiles, with his people";
and again,
"Praise the Lord, all Gentiles,
  and let all the peoples praise him";
and further Isaiah says,
"The root of Jesse shall come,
he who rises to rule the Gentiles;
in him shall the Gentiles hope."

May the God of hope fill you with all joy and peace in believing, so that by the power of the Holy Spirit you may abound in hope.

Romans 15:4–13, RSV

Father, here we are. What should we say to you? You know us. You know how we are and what we do wrong. You know us better than we know our'selves. You know the weakness of our hearts, and that we are so discouraged and tired. You know how confused we are. You have expected us too much to respond with faith and hope and love toward everyone. Now have patience with us. Do not reject us, where we have laid guilt on ourselves and have become contemptible. Do not look at our deeds and omissions. Look at us with the eyes of hope so that we may awaken and praise you as well as we can. Let your light illumine our obscurity as it illuminated the world on Easter morning.

"The God of Hope"—so Paul called the Lord our God here. That is indeed a fortunate name. The uniqueness of the God of the Bible cannot be said more to the point. There are many gods in the religions of the nations and many idols in our lives. But these are gods without hope and idols without future. They stand at the border of life like watchdogs and sentries and oppress us with anxiety and care. They want to be the guarantee of fortune and security, but they impoverish man in the search for pleasure and fulfillment and let him return empty. The God of the Bible, however, is the God of hope. He encounters us in his promises, and attracts us into his rich future. To have this God and to catch hold of new hope belong in one breath.

To catch hold of a hope which makes the heart wide, but signifies freedom and obtains space, recognizes the path toward the future and smells the morning air over a day which is becoming gray. Therefore, we can say further: the God of hope is the God of freedom. In him no boundaries are set nor does he set any. He breaks through defenses of anxiety and the walls of care. He breaks through boundaries which we ourselves have set in order to distinguish ourselves from other men and to affirm ourselves. He breaks into the boundary of our solitude in which we have hidden so that no one will come near us. He steps over the boundary of race, in which man loathes man, and the boundaries of class and strata in society. He despises the difference between black and white, poor and rich, educated and uneducated; for he seeks men—poor, suffering, hating and ugly, cramped and stunted men—and accepts them as they are. That knowledge makes us free and is a source of support. We can hope in him—the God of freedom.

If now the freedom of God is visible in the overstepping of our boundaries, then finally we must also say: this God of hope is the boundless God. Whoever hears of him, thinks of him, prays to him is grasped by hope. And whomever hope grasps becomes free, and whoever becomes thus free over-steps boundaries and breaks through limits. Whoever obtains what this hope promises stops at nothing, has no rest until all boundaries are broken, until every corner of the earth and every impulse of our bodies are permeated with the promises of God and free and ready to obtain his joy.

Nevertheless, how can we hope with "full hope," with a hope which "overflows"?

Naturally we would gladly be more hopeful in our work and more confident with our fellow-men. But there are simple limits, limits of strength, in the possibilities of others and of hard reality. We would gladly give ourselves to this hope, but the relationships are not that way. Is a man young? In his hopes, the young man overshoots the goal. Only later does he note what is reality and what is not. Then he thinks, "Hoping and waiting makes many fools." Leaving the future alone, he blinks only skeptically into the new day: let it come! Now he considers himself a realist; all possibilities are played through. A tired smirk moves the corners of his mouth; and before he becomes cynical, he says: *bonjour tristesse!* Welcome, sweet sadness, resigned boredom! We know life; nothing fools us. We have found nothing in it that could give rise to a wider hope, nothing that one should stand up for. Take it as it comes and be still.

Is it different with us who are called by the God of hope? Certainly some go out "beyond the limits" of the church and their home into foreign lands—missionaries in India, Africa; doctors and engineers in developmental help. Certainly many go "over the boundary" from Sunday worship and Christian customs and do something unexpected in politics. They protest against public breach of law and social wrongs. They hunger after true righteousness and stand up for reconciliation, understanding, and peace among races, peoples, and social partners who are full of hate.

But mostly one sees nothing special being done by those who are called by the God of hope, no boundaries being stepped over, but rather the painful observance of boundaries and competition in that society where they live. Their hope has become a vain promise to them and their mobilizing power lost. Then hope crosses no more boundaries nor any longer makes free, but lets man get by harmlessly within them. Only this is not entirely harmless for it is the source of much sin. No, I do not mean the sins of evil and of pride where we want to "be like God." Who would be so presumptuous; indeed, who would make such an effort? I mean the unapparent but oppressing sins of omission. It is not the great evil we do but the good we omit that condemns us. Why do we remain so guilty before our neighbors? It is because, when we needed to do something for them, we had no hope; because, when we should have made something happen, we did not think it would work. "It is not our sins so much as our despair which ruins us," said the church father Chrysostom.

So many doubts and considerations come to us in this way. Hope is indeed the obtaining of all understanding and powers for the promising future. Where this direction is confounded, our thoughts also become confused. Rather than direct themselves to the future and to what should happen, they return—coming back on us, they eat away what still is in us until nothing more is there, what could not just as well be different, and everything becomes equal. Doubt is only a hope which has lost its object and which now begins to devour itself. Thus, there is always still a little hope in doubt. It is just that we have become so small, giving up at every limit we encounter, no longer feeling ourselves capable and losing not only hope but freedom and, with both, God himself. Then no longer does the Christian carry before men the torch of hope, but only trails behind him a sad consolation.

But where can we learn that hope again? Paul gives us two very simple hints:

1. We learn hope in the Bible, and
2. We may hope since Christ has received us.

1. We can go out into the world in order to learn fear. We encounter it in the small unpleasantnesses of the ordinary day, in human insufficiencies, in sickness, and in death. But this is why we read the Bible—in order to learn hope in vexation, monotony, and fear, and the daily degradations. For to what purpose is that all written there, and to what purpose is it narrated and preached: the calling forth of creation out of nothing, the setting out of Abraham, the journey of Israel out of Egypt, the incarnation of Jesus and his resurrection from death, the sending out of the disciples to all people. To what purpose is all of that? Paul says: "Whatever was written in former days was written for our instruction, that by steadfastness and by the encouragement of the scriptures, we might have hope" (Rom. 15:4). Over the history which the Bible tells, and out of which it speaks, is stretched the wide arch of

God's promises. In these promises men learn hope and also the patience of hope as they break open the landscape of the future thus opened to them. They come out of the history of God and they go expectantly into it—as he has said to them. They cross over the boundaries of all they now have and presently experience. Out of this history, we have heard Isaiah's promises for the future. To his fatigued and destroyed people he announced the Messiah and the spring of his peaceful kingdom for the entire parched creation: "He will arise and rule over the heathen. On him will the heathen hope." Out of this history comes also the Letter to the Romans. There Paul sees the church of Jesus as the fulfillment of the hope of the prophet for the praise of the heathen, and he places us also in this hope. The Bible is the textbook of hope, and the best presupposition for the theology and church of today to understand it correctly is this: every page and every word is concerned with the burning question, What may I hope?

2. We cannot force hopes on ourselves or on anyone else. Before we come to hope, we must first have the narrow confines made wide so that we can breathe freely. We must first obtain new possibilities and a new outlook and vision before we can hope. In order to hope we need to be loved a little and have the knowledge that there is one who hopes in, waits on, answers for, and believes in us. "Accept one another just as Christ has accepted you, to the praise of God," Paul states. This is the basis of hope, he says, and the breadth of the horizon in which hope exists. With the resurrection of Jesus, God has accepted us, just as one accepts and brings to honor something which is lost and believed forgotten. What did Isaiah say of the Messiah? "He will not judge those that see his eyes nor speak righteousness to those that hear his ears. He will judge the poor with righteousness and the suffering in the land of justice with mercy." Does this not happen where Jesus is with tax collectors and sinners? Does

this not happen where his gospel makes the godless righteous? Does this not take place there where the God of hope places himself before those who are "without God and without hope in the world"? He is the God of hope because he has hope for us and practices the patience of hope with us. And whatever may always be wrong with us, we are the hope of God in this world. In the business world we often say, "That young man is full of hope. We can expect something of him." Then we count on his good results. God, however, makes us hope differently. He makes us hope because he has patience with us—boundless, untiring patience. His hope, born out of the dust, cannot perish in the dust of our everyday. Born out of the resurrection, it cannot therefore be exhausted in the cross of our lives. Born out of death, it breaks up therefore the iron rings of anxiety and of uselessness.

For what does this hope hope? The answer is easily said but difficult to practice: it hopes for all, and it hopes for everything.

It hopes for all men. That is what Isaiah meant: "The root of Jesse shall come to rule the Gentiles, and in him shall they hope." Paul cites this prophecy in his letter. How narrow-minded we are in our faith, and considerate only of ourselves. We would like to believe and we cannot do it. Why not? Because even in believing we still seek only ourselves. How can we believe without taking in one another? How can we believe without having faith and without hoping for the Indian, the Chinese, the Buddhist, and the Communist? If we are pious we say, "I take Jesus as my Savior." In the Bible, it is not so. There it says: "I believe in Jesus, the Lord of the World."—"On him the heathen hope." If they are not all saved for the praise of God, then we also are not saved. If they do not all come to the peace of God, then we also find no peace, for there are those in the world who would be less than we. Paul sighs with the entire waiting creation. How can we then sigh only for ourselves? "On him will the heathen hope." Why do they not yet do it? Is it not because we have not yet accepted them? If we comprehend that only a little, then the mission yields itself. But then we do not put in motion the mission. For Christianity *is* mission. "Mission is the infection with hope," said the Dutchman Hans Hoekendijk. Where Christianity begins to accept men, that is, to hope for all men, pray for all men, and recognize that all are responsible, there begins the infection of the heathen with hope.

But then this hope goes for all, namely, for the peace of the entire dismembered creation. "The wolves will lie with the lambs and children will play with the serpents," says Isaiah in a vivid picture. If hope is to go to that point, how can we look on peacefully when there is enmity, hate and contempt, degradation and offense in this creation? Mission is then also the infection of public life in society and politics with hope. It is the service of reconciliation, the gift of peace and respect, the battle against unrighteousness and deeds of violence, the furtherance of life, fortune, and health. Mission then is a service in that future of life which God had promised. God hopes for everything. His joy will also be a totally evident, bodily, ecumenical, and political joy in his creation. Mission is then hope in action.

Whoever makes a man laugh again unlocks for him the heavenly kingdom.

Whoever gives a man patience infects him with hope.

Whoever accepts a man as he himself is accepted by Christ loosens his tongue for praise.

Let us march forth from our customs and our habits in order to learn hope in the Bible. Let us set out and overrun the boundaries that we may infect life with hope.

Let us no longer respect boundaries, but only that which opens boundaries.

Father, we know that we cannot come to you without

our brother. Thus, we pray not for ourselves, but for those who are near and far, friends and enemies. We pray to you for grace for the indifferent and the tired, for the small of faith and the hopeless. We pray to you for patience for the godless, for the heathen, for the atheistic. We ask you for that light of your hope for Israel so that it will recognize your Messiah. We ask you for the coming of your kingdom and its fullness for the hungry in India and South America. We ask you for the coming of your righteousness for the degraded and the offended. We ask you for the arrival of your freedom for the oppressed. Let nothing which serves your future be brought to defeat. Let us find patience with our neighbors, and give us the courage to practice daily the art of hoping in patience. Lord, let your kingdom come and this world pass away.

3

Look, Everything Has Become New

Therefore, if any one is in Christ, he is a new creation; the old has passed away, behold, the new has come. All this is from God, who through Christ reconciled us to himself and gave us the ministry of reconciliation; that is, God was in Christ reconciling the world to himself, not counting their trespasses against them, and entrusting to us the message of reconciliation. So we are ambassadors for Christ, God making his appeal through us. We beseech you on behalf of Christ, be reconciled to God. For our sake he made him to be sin who knew no sin, so that in him we might become the righteousness of God.

2 Corinthians 5:17–21, RSV

In Bert Brecht's *Kalendergeschichten* [Calendar Stories], a man whom Mr. Keuner had not seen for a long time greeted him with the words, "You have not changed at all." "Oh," said Mr. Keuner, and grew pale.

In the text of the apostle Paul, we are greeted with the words: "If any one is in Christ, he is a new creation; the old has passed away, behold, the new has come." It is as if Paul

were to say the opposite of the man Mr. Keuner encountered: "You have completely changed." That would be
ground enough, I think, still to say a confused "Oh," and to
grow even paler. Are we then "new men"? Has "the old"
actually "passed away"? Where has "everything become
new"?

If we look in the mirror in the morning, we can only
confirm that the old is still there and becoming always older.
If we look at the men with whom we live, it is seldom otherwise. They are as they were. If we look in our environment
we find that it too is not quite new. It is soiled. Prices rise;
social suffering in the Third World grows; tension-filled affairs
all over the world bring unending trouble. How shall that
become new? Where and to whom am I a new creation? How
can this old threatened world with its unsolved problems be
habitable and homelike?

Now Paul was no visionary, no optimistic fanatic who
viewed everything through rose-colored glasses. His life was
too much characterized by pain for that. What reason can he
have, therefore, for this shocking assertion that we and everything around us have become new?

It is as if he were to lead us before a mirror of which we
had never before known, a mirror in which we see ourselves
with different eyes, and which shows us our new face. It is
the mirror of the crucified Christ. In him we see ourselves no
longer with the eyes of a particular conceit, proud or sad;
but as life has made us, with the eyes of love—with the eyes
of a love which does not criticize but liberates, which will
make nothing out of us but loves us as we are.

Man sees himself only in mirrors and in masks. In the Greek
saga, the youth Narcissus once came to some water where
he saw his own image and loved himself. Our vanities and our
deep depressions result from the self-love that resides in all of
us. We are anxious for our life and for our honor; we are
incapable of loving and incapable of mourning. Is anyone in

Christ? Then he is no longer such a Narcissus. He forgets himself, for he experiences himself as loved, accepted, reconciled—as a new creature, as a creation of love. The old has passed away. He no longer needs to seek himself, for today and tomorrow and in eternity he is found. Certainly in the morning he still sees the old face there in the mirror, but he can look beyond himself. He can laugh at his vanities and his anxieties, for he has gained distance from himself. He lives, as Paul says, "henceforth, no more himself." He knows that he is of infinitely greater value to another and greater one—namely, of just as much value as the death of Christ was costly to God. He no longer needs to prove his worth to himself and to others. He is free as one who experiences a great love is free.

Albrecht Dürer painted a picture of Christ which became a self-portrait. Seeing himself in the Crucified One, he found himself safe and free in the sorrow of his love.

Whoever learns to see himself thus in the mirror of the cross also obtains new eyes. He sees his neighbors and his surroundings differently. "Look," says Paul. "Open your eyes wide and look into this mirror. Everything has become new." Luther wrote amazing words about that: "The sins of the entire world are not there where they are vivid and are felt. For theology, there is no sin, no death in the world; but for reason, sin is nowhere more evident than in the world. It is entirely and wholly godless. True doctrine says, in fact, that there is no sin in the world since Christ has conquered this sin in his body." One might say that the reverse must be true since reason wants to improve the world and faith often enough only sighs over this veil of tears and deplores the sins of the non-Christian society. That is not faith. Whoever would look at sin, his own shortcomings, the evil of others, and the baseness of social and political relationships with the eye of God must find them uncovered and overthrown in the cross. And in so doing, he sees the world as free—free from sin, free from anger, and free from evil death. Look, everything has become new.

Actually everything? How has it with the suffering of sick children? How has it with the fate of the old about whom no one is concerned? We read in the mirror of the newspapers about millions of murdered and starving Bengalis, three million Afghans looking for water, one million North Vietnamese drowned in floods, and so on. And we can do so little. Has all that become different?

Yes, all this also has fundamentally and thoroughly become new. What an illusion, we want to say. Is it not realistic to feel righteous anger over so much injustice? "Who is guilty?" we ask, if we hear of something like this and want to eradicate it. Righteous anger is, in fact, realistic; and if anyone has a reason for it, it is surely God himself. But God does not play the angry game with us; we do not find God there where our anger, in order to become absolute and penetrating, seeks his anger. In the death of Christ, the protest of his anger against evil has become the sacrifice of love for the malicious and the forsaken. That is the great return in God himself, the revolution in God of which the entire New Testament speaks.

Whoever sees the world with these eyes no longer nails down evil on its malice. He no longer seeks after the guilty but accepts the suffering in their sorrow, for he sees them together with God and at one with reconciliation. He does not accuse their reality, but reckons with them the new possibilities which are waiting in their reconciliation with God, and he participates in their comfort. He sees the relations no longer only as they are, but together with their new future. He sees them in the messianic light of their reconciliation as a new creation, "free from sin and death, free from anger and power."

Whoever stands in the dawn of the new day of God shall not fight against the long shadows of night, but hold himself in the light. That is more dangerous to the shadows than the battle against the shadows. To see reality means to see the world from the cross of Christ. Then scales fall from the eyes: "Look, the new is there. Look, the future has already begun. Look, the day has come near." All that has become possible in the person Jesus. Let us therefore already do today what shall be tomorrow. The world is no longer a hopeless case, and in the final time there are no longer any hopeless cases. One can become hope for the other since God through Christ became hope for us all.

Nevertheless many among us will still say: "It could be that one who is right in Christ and believes quite firmly can experience this and see the world with such enlightened eyes, but who is already in Christ?" Here to be sure is a yearning after a faith which renews everything; but not faith itself, rather insecurity and uncertainty.

We must not falsely attribute this certainty to us. It does not come from men, but, as Paul continues, "All this is from God." And we should take God more seriously than we do ourselves and our idols and demons. For, "God was in Christ reconciling the world to himself." The last secret is not his wrath and silence which makes life dark for us as we have so often experienced it; but it is entirely and wholly at one with the proclaimed devotion of Jesus, his way into death for the life of the world as we perceive it in faith. The God whom we seek above in heaven, or in the depth of our heart, or in the path of world history, does not give it. We meet there only the wish-makers and the anxious dreams which we make ourselves. God is there where man has not sought him, but despised and rejected him. God is in that man from Nazareth, who, without power and nobility, died outside at the gates of society.

What did God do there in that man whose last word cried out: "My God, why have you forsaken me?" He gave himself in the pain of love and bore a hopeless death upon himself. What did he do there in that despised one? He took our contempt upon himself, my coldness of heart also. What did he do there in that suffering one? He took the suffering of the world on himself, and my sadness also. In the suffering and death of Jesus, he did not rest so that we could say, "Look, God is silent"; God was creative in this pure suffering and pain of Jesus in the highest way. He "reconciled the world with himself," says Paul. "He did not account to them their sin," he continues; and further, "He has made him who knew no sin to be sin for us so that we become through him, the righteous of God." All our unrighteousness is on him and all his righteousness is with us; all our impurity with him and all his purity with us; all our anger and grief with him and all his creative joy with us. That is what reconciliation means.

And if it is true that God has reconciled "the world" with himself, who then is excluded? Who then is not in Christ as long as he belongs to this world? It is not up to our faith or to our unfaith, our high or low feelings. God reconciled the world in Christ. Thus all who live and die in this world are included. No one is excluded. Indeed, before we believe or doubt, before we are grasped by it or even feel nothing, this reconciliation has happened in us and for us. For God—God himself—was in the forsaken Christ and became the forsaken God and Father. In that he came nearer to us than we are to ourselves, or could come to another man.

Nothing is too high in God that could not be near, tangible, and clear with everyone in the story of Christ. Nothing is so hidden in man that it could not be made public and accessible here in Christ. "God in Christ"—one scarcely ventures to speak it out, for it means, "We are the righteousness of God in the world. We are new men of a new creation." Then we turn around and find that others no longer are in hell, but we see Christ in them as he waits on us.

God lets us participate in the reconciliation of the world. Not that we must also make our contribution to this reconciliation, for then reconciliation would be in bad hands; however, he lets us participate in the service of reconciliation to this unsaved world. He does not make us accusers of other men, of the bad, godless society, but agents of reconciliation in this society.

What shall we do? No one can be forced into freedom. One can only be invited and asked to reconciliation. Thus God asks, not commands, us to reconciliation. It is an honor to be asked, for the request already gives something of the freedom to which we are invited. We perceive in the invitation that we are of value to another. The person who makes a request has no great power. He forces none and compels no one, but he opens the door to new and entirely different possibilities or reconciling love. Lords command. Judges judge. Party leaders proclaim authoritative solutions. Many Christians force others to their form of belief. God in Christ, however, asks, invites, opens the door, and creates free life. Whoever is disgusted with commands and orders, with advertising slogans and accusations, knows of reconciliation's entreaty to value this call of freedom: be reconciled with God, with the God of freedom. Pressure is not in reconciliation. Run no longer, therefore, to those who want to set you under pressure in politics or in the church.

The service of reconciliation has its price, nevertheless. Reconciliation cost God dearly, as the cross of Jesus makes clear. It can have nothing to do with weak tolerance and the appeasing of disputants. Reconciliation is also not gentle goodness and bittersweet indulgence. It demands— as is seen in the life and death of Paul—the full use of a life which lives no longer to itself alone, but stands in the service of a greater.

The word of reconciliation has come into the world through Christianity, but so often it is misused and betrayed by Christians and the church. Can one believe Christians to be in the service of reconciliation if they do not practice it concretely as Jesus did in healing the sick, casting out demons, and sitting at the table with sinners and traitors? In this way, and not otherwise, does he also reach us, so that we may recognize ourselves in them and meet them in the community of reconciliation. Jesus himself proclaimed the kingdom to the poor, but not only to the poor. He proclaimed it to the rich also. He was a friend of lepers and of the irreconciled, not of the self-satisfied and self-righteous. His mission brought reconciliation to all men exactly in that he strongly sided with the hopeless and with those who were discriminated against. For that reason, he died between two criminals of this society.

The power of reconciliation has a real, changing character. It has nothing to do with religious veiling of irreconcilable conflicts, but is that power which is made powerful in the weak.

The world is bad; therefore, it must be changed, many say. The world is reconciled; therefore, it *can* be changed, say those who hope. Certainly we ask: Which actions shall we initiate? Where can we do something appropriate? Don't let us flee blindly into action, but let us first recognize and learn to see. Necessary actions are then not far away. Let us recognize that we have, in that Crucified One, become a new creation of love—and are no longer the old. Let us see the world with those new eyes of its reconciliation. And not only the world in its entirety, but also simply the men with whom we live and work. They too are no longer the old ones. "Look, everything has become new."

How was that in the beginning? "You have not changed at all," said the man to Mr. Keuner, and Mr. Keuner turned pale. What would have happened to Mr. Keuner if the man had said, "Mr. Keuner, you have changed completely; you are a new creature"? If one accepts him as such and would live thus with him, would not everything then actually become new? Would not life then be full of surprises? If we venture to believe, then we will see the wonder of God: the miracle of reconciliation.

Eternal God, merciful Father, we thank you for your creation. Everything that is there is gladly there, and thanks you in all joy for its existence. We then thank you also for the joy in life and the fortune of love and friendship. Still more, we thank you for your new creation. You have found us in the pain of your love where we only sought ourselves. You are the forsaken God and Father. Those whom we avoid and despise, you have made your friends. Open our eyes so that we see the reconciliation which has happened in us and in the world. Open our eyes for your reconciled new creation. In the name of Jesus, we ask you for the service of reconciliation to the irreconciled, for the persecuted and those who persecute them, for the exploited and those who exploit them, for those whose race is discriminated against and those who despise them. Lord, we wait on your new creation as we believe your reconciliation of the world. And if you can also use us for that, then let our good will and our mission please you. Bless the words with which we attempt to reach the troubled, the sick, and the silent. Bless the political and social work to the disadvantaged.

4

The Resurrection of the Crucified

The resurrection of Christ is controversial. Many no longer know what they should make of it. It did not take place in the world of calculable and available things. Is it an event among other events, which were and are? Is it a symbol from the language of a far time, with which Christians of that time expressed what value Jesus was to them? Can one prove that something happened to Jesus, even though in our experience nothing similar happens?

In such affairs one person doubts and the other saves his faith in the biblical self-assertion: it is so, since it is written thus in the Bible.

Are these alternatives the last word?

In the early church, as the New Testament documents, the resurrection of Christ stood as the central point. Faith was the hope of resurrection. The Christian remembered everything that Jesus had done and spoken because his death was not his end, but his resurrection was his true beginning. He expected from Christ the fulfillment of everything God had promised: freedom, righteousness, peace, and finally a splendid, beautiful life which no longer knew death. These were his thoughts every Sunday morning in remembrance and expectation of the reawakening of the crucified Christ. But even in the ancient church that interest in the resurrection festival was soon driven out of place by Christmas, the festival of the Incarnation of God. The Reformation and Pietism placed the Passion and the Cross of Christ in the foreground. Only since the Enlightenment has this celebration of the death gained significance. How did this displaced event come to be in the center of Christian faith?

Strange to say, it goes parallel with the shifting of the direction of the eyes of faith from hope to remembrance, from future to the past, from history which comes and realizes something new to eternity which always is. For the New Testament, the resurrection of Jesus from the dead means always the beginning of the general resurrection of the dead and the arrival of the messianic kingdom of freedom from guilt and death. As Jesus is resurrected from the dead, then will the dead live, the guilty be acquitted, enemies reconciled, and the suffering made happy. For the disciples this fulfillment of the messianic hope appeared to be nearly within grasp with the appearance of the resurrected Christ. If they thought of him, they thought of the future. Their faith in Christ was their hope for this future, and their hope for this future became a certainty through their faith in Christ.

Nevertheless, when the hope that this future would come, and was already quite near, lost itself in the shifting sands of history, their faith changed also: the resurrected Christ was no longer the beginning and present of such a future of God for the earth, but he was the eternal one, the spiritual one, the man who is elevated to God. They believed they would come with him into heaven, but they no longer hoped to obtain with him the future of a new earth. They believed in the redemption of the soul from the pain of the body, but

THE GOSPEL OF LIBERATION

they no longer hoped for the redemption of the oppressed body. Easter meant only that there is a life after death. With such appearances of the disintegration of hope, the understanding of Easter and resurrection were also lost. Christianity, which began by infecting mankind as a messianic and missionary movement with hope and proclamations of freedom, changed itself into a world religion which secured for man the most precious goods of eternity.

This time is coming to an end today. Christians must therefore attempt to recollect their origins, their mobilizing power, and their actual commission. It appears to me that it does not lie in awakening religious feeling and bringing men to faith in God, but in bringing about with the message of the resurrection of the Crucified that power of hope which makes one ready to take up the cross of love leading to a life of freedom. Easter cannot only mean that there is a life after death. That sounds like an empty promise. Easter must mean that life here is already changed; it becomes free from many oppressions, from guilt and anxiety of death.

If we want to penetrate deeper, then we must ask what the New Testament actually meant by the expression "Resurrection of the Dead." It was not something wholly wonderful that happened only to Jesus, but had bound with it definite hopes and expectations for oneself and for all men. First of all, this expression is a simile by which something incomparable is meant: as one is awakened from sleep and then lifts himself up and arises, so shall it be experienced by those who must suffer death. The familiar process of being waked up when it is time to get up serves to express a completely unfamiliar event and a destiny as yet not experienced which first awaits the dead.

One sees immediately that this simile is entirely inadequate. When one awakens in the morning he returns to his old life; he accepts the work, worry, and guilt where he had laid it aside the evening before. We often fall asleep and wake up again. With death, however, that is at an end. It is final. One does not "fall asleep," as it is often expressed in order to cover up the harshness of dying, but one ceases to live. "Resurrection of the dead" does also not mean that one is "given again to life," for this life is at an end. "Resurrection of the dead" can also not mean that a sleeping life will again be awakened, for where everything is dead nothing can any longer be reawakened. The expression, taken from our daily experiences, does, however, serve as a symbol for something we have not yet experienced.

And what is that?

What is meant is a life out of death that is no longer degraded by death. Resurrection of the dead is thus not the return of a dead one into this life that comes to an end in death, but simply a new life that has death behind it. This new life consists not in the awakening of a sleeping person, but—and this is as Paul meant it—by a new creation of God which calls the nonbeing into existence, makes the dead alive as he calls the world out of nothing into life. On what do those wait who hope for resurrection? They wait on a new creation of God. They wait on a life and a life relationship for whom God and then also men will be able to say: "Look, everything is very good, for it is all become new!" Death is no more. Guilt is forgiven; evil is overthrown. Sorrow has transformed itself into happiness and tears into laughter.

All this has happened for the disciples in the Easter appearances of Jesus. That man who died in the night of forsakenness by God and man they saw in the splendor of the advent of this new creation of God. What happened to him, then, whom they saw die and who encountered them in a manner so difficult to comprehend? No one was there; no one saw it. Out of the whole substance of their notions there is only this one thing: he is resurrected from the dead; with him begins that new creation of the world: freedom from the degradation of death. He lives and we also shall

live. A new future from God begins to fulfill itself in a godless world. Meanwhile the disciples say: he, Christ, is resurrected. They tie their hope of the future with their knowledge
of Christ and their perception of Christ with their expectation
of the future. It is understandable, therefore, when men to
whom the future offers no occasion for hope also cannot
make much of the resurrection of Christ. Where the future is
dark, Christ is forced to be dark, also, and, conversely, where
Christ is no longer believed, the future is dark.

Naturally we still have the feeling that all conceptions of
the future and, even more, of a future after death, are
dreams, fantasies, and speculations. We know nothing definite of the future and we had better not believe anyone
who claims that he knows something of it. How shall we
speak then of the future which is not yet there? How can we
speak of future history when we have not yet been there?
What will pictures of life after death do for us if we still have
to endure life? It gives us hope everywhere, at all times,
we say. Man hopes so long as he lives. He is never finished
unless he becomes tired and unsuccessful and death does him
in.

What should therefore be special in this hope of Christians?
Wherein lies its basis? However little we obtain faith out of
ourselves and love without being loved, so little does this
hope have its basis in the voices of youth or the processes of
history. It has its basis outside itself in a deed wherein God is
present—the act of divine mercy. Our mercy consists mostly in
that we have empathy with the sorrowful and that we alleviate
misery. The mercy of God, however, is a creating act which
brings the new into the world. He calls the nonbeing into
being, makes the dead living, secures justice for those lacking
justice, and life for the dying. Otherwise he would not be
"God." That the mercy of God is perceived in the resurrection of the crucified Christ and in the rebirth of the hopeless (1 Pet. 1:3) is not opinion of God but history which is

open to the future. The iron ring which death locks around this life is sprung open in this history: in Jesus through resurrection into life—in us through the tumult and revolt into living hope.

Hope thus founded in the victory of life over death places the whole man as by birth into a new life. That is the hope of resurrection. It goes beyond the scope of possibilities for it sets itself in opposition to the strongest contradiction of life and its hope here: death. It advances the claim that God himself is against death and has its basis for this boldness in the resurrection of Christ by God. Therefore, it is an indestructible and eternal hope. We would grossly misuse the Christian hope if we made it the playground of all our unfulfilled wishes. Then it would actually be only a vain comfort. Christian hope, however, does not speak of anyone's future. It speaks only of Christ and his future. The name of Christ is no empty title, but designates the basis and the reality of this hope. The New Testament never says simply that Christ is resurrected and that a noble future for all men is now beginning. It speaks always of the resurrection only in connection with his cross, and therefore of hope always in connection with the sorrow and patience of love.

Not every life gives occasion for hope, only this life of Jesus which in love took the cross and death on itself. In this death came resurrection. In this death everything that does not affirm in human life what is evil, inhuman, and against God becomes public. In his resurrection originates then a passion of hope which accepts such sorrow. It does not realize itself in empty dreams of the future, but always and only in contradiction against the visible realities of godlessness and inhumanity. The dreams of the future innately depreciate the present. Man lives with his thoughts in an unreality which is not yet and perhaps never will be. Christian hope, on the contrary, however, draws the future here into the present, for it becomes that future of God which is present in the crucified Christ. Here it arrives. It exists here, in the now.

It would indeed be no contradiction if man were to say: here is one life, and after death comes another life. Both such lives, separated by death, would have nothing to say. But that would not be a living hope, only deferment and adjournment. Hope would not be living until the future becomes present, and the present does not let itself remain as it is. Hope for a life after death does not make one alive; only hope against death does this. The hope of resurrection proves its truth in the actual contradiction of true life against a life of death, in contradiction of righteousness against evil, and of peace against disruption. It does not lead to the point that men are satisfied with relations as they are. It is not only a comfort in a toilsome and judged-for-death life.

The resurrection of Christ from the dead is also a protest against death, and against the degradation of men through sorrow. Paul calls death "the last enemy" of God and of men (1 Cor. 15:26). On the contrary, the resurrecting Christ and hope must be understood as the enemy of death and of a world which has established itself with death.

It is not only that man wants to be like God, which makes us miserable, but still more that he does not want to be the man God has called him to be. From hopelessness, despondency, laziness, and sadness arises the frustration of a life which scarcely wants to participate, which does not know what it should make of itself, and which lets itself be impelled. Not only the evil that one does, but even more, the good that one does not do, makes man guilty. Our omissions accuse us; they accuse us of the lack of hope. Hopelessness can always have two forms. It can be presumption, and it can be doubt. Presumption is an untimely, self-willed anticipation of what is hoped for by God. Doubt is just as arbitrary an anticipation that what is hoped for is unfulfillable. Both rise against the sorrow of hope. Both want their fulfillment now, or no hope at all.

Doubt in hope does not necessarily need to show a doubtful face. It can be the mere silencing absence of mind, outlook, future, and intention. It can have the face of a laughing resignation. Let the world pass by! It is nothing. There is, it appears to me, scarcely a way of behaving so widespread in the products of decay of a resigned Christianity and following it into a post-Christian world, as this sadness—this knowing sadness—this irrelevant game with faded hope. "Think clearly and do not hope" is, to be sure, the role of the brave hero of our time—Sisyphus. But does that thinking obtain clarity, and that behaving sense, without the horizon and without the power of hope?!

Doubt in the future can also promise fortune: "Why ramble in the distance? Look, the good lies so near. Learn only to grasp fortune, for fortune is always there," wrote Goethe. He considers hope as deception and a vexation which keeps man from being totally present, and wholly fortunate in being so. "We never consider ourselves in the present. We pass by the future as if it came too slowly. We remember the past in order to detain it, since it disappears so fast. Thus, we never live but always hope to live, and thus it is inevitable that we become happy in the expectation that there is nothing," complained Pascal. We would gladly shake off the burden of hope in order to give ourselves entirely to the pleasure of the present. The person who lives eternally in the future is never there; he is always somewhere else. Hoping to live can be something great, but it can also be a rather deep unreality.

Again, we must reflect on the fact that Christian hope does not originate out of a dreaming game with unreal possibilities, but represents a passion which is born out of suffering. Is there then a condition in the present which is untroubled and eternal? Must we not forget what was and what is to be, forget what others suffer, in order to rejoice about our own fortunes? To be entirely present, the eternal present of God —that is also the fortune on which the Christian hope hopes. That would be salvation, in which everything is healed and whole and good and perfect.

But so long as guilt is there with which man makes himself and others unhappy, so long as death is a power which plunges all happiness into decay, we must shut our eyes in order to see the present as happy and healing. Happiness and fullness and true life are for the hope which holds eyes open, here first hidden in that Christ who bears guilt, suffering, and the death of the world in his love. Therefore, this hope does not praise the rich happily, but the poor, the suffering, the degraded and insulted, the guilt-laden and the dying, as it appears in the blissful praises of Jesus and is guaranteed in his resurrection. We do not become happy by shutting our eyes to the sorrow of the suffering, but, in love for the lost, taking their work and suffering on ourselves. But for that, we need patience, we need hope. And patience *is* the art of daily hoping.

The New Testament always speaks of the "patience of hope." "If we hope for what we have not seen, then we wait on it with patience," says Paul. Still, what kind of patience is that? Patience out of resignation would be hopelessness. Patience out of hope is something entirely different. The patience of Christian hope has its basis and its image in the patience of Jesus, in his love, and in his giving up of himself. In a more general way, we can say it thus: true patience allows the other man time. It gives him freedom. It takes into account his possibilities, including the possibilities of God not yet awakened within, and thus it gives him a future. It does not only take man as he is. It does not blackmail him with demands as he should be. It has hope for the other and opens to him possibilities of changing himself. It "gives him a chance," as one says. It makes him free. In the patience of hoping, the coming freedom forces itself into the unredeemed world. The resurrection of Christ is the basis for the stance of patience and confidence against an impatient and disheartened world.

No one grasps the means and the content of reality of the resurrection who does not keep in mind the purpose and the future which is initiated therein. Not in defense and accommodation, but only in attack and in advance upon the goal of eternal life and the kingdom of God is the resurrection of Christ demonstrable. The world for which we are born is circumscribed by transitoriness and by death. Only the inner rebirth of hope and the external event of the liberation of the world grasps the significance of the Easter event. If we take for the Easter event the future for which it speaks, then it becomes silent. If faith looks anxiously back, then it becomes mute. Easter is an event which opens up the future. We understand its reality only in the living hope which thrusts us into what is hoped for itself (Luther).

5

CALL TO FREEDOM

For you were called to freedom, brethren; only do not use your freedom as an opportunity for the flesh, but through love be servants of
one another. For the whole law is fulfilled in one word, "You shall
love your neighbor as yourself." But if you bite and devour one another take heed that you are not consumed by one another.

Galatians 5:13–15, RSV

If one asks what a Christian is and what is expected from
him, the answers are mostly negative: a Christian is one who
does not smoke, does not drink, does not commit adultery, is
not indecent. He does not protest, he does not rebel, he
wastes neither money nor time. That means he does nothing that many might occasionally, perhaps gladly, do once.
The impression that a Christian man is a free man who dis-
seminates liberation is seldom publicly generated. Religion
resounds after commitment, and faith after obedience. It is
understandable that the liberation movements of the modern
world often demand freedom from religion along with free-

dom from lordship and exploitation. Understandable too is the child's reaction when he discovers his own age. Since it cramps him, he casts off the mantle of religion and obedience which has protected him to that point and sings with glowing eyes: "I loosen all chains and say no, no, no." Churches are terrified when such freedoms are demanded. Christian parents no longer understand their children when they say no.

For Paul, freedom has an entirely different appearance. For him, faith itself begins with a liberation such as the world has not yet seen. For him, the entire gospel is a message of freedom. Therefore, our chapter begins with his call "Thus stand only in the freedom to which Christ has called us" and his further repeat "You are called to freedom."

Have no anxiety before freedom! Do not make yourselves again into slaves! Whoever hears the call to freedom has faith. Faith is not well designated as an "absolute feeling of dependence," if, by that, submissiveness is intended, but is much more an "absolute feeling of freedom" in communion with the free God. "Everything is yours. You are Christ's: Christ is God's," says Paul in 1 Corinthians 3:21-23.

Now such freedom can cause dizziness and call forth fear of misuse. First, we are called to freedom. We do not have it simply as a hereditary factor in itself, or as a possession already in our pocket. To be sure, Schiller saw it that "man is free and he was born in chains." But in fact he is first free when the chains fall. If we are called to freedom, then there is something that man is missing and that comes to him first in the call to liberation. Without tangible liberation, there is no freedom. It is no title of possession and no privilege, but a surprising event which grasps unfree man so that he breathes freely and laughs and stirs and moves himself with new power.

A call to freedom leads the way to freedom, for we cannot be forced or sentenced to freedom. The call opens up our freedom to answer. It attracts, it calls, it invites; it summons and reverberates from the freedom to which it attracts and invites.

A call is usually a command, however. One is called to his office, called to his obligations. How can one be called to freedom? We must remember that in the Bible more is intended with such a call. It is a creative call. Thus when God calls, "Let there be light, and there was light," he summons the nonbeing into being (Rom. 4:17). Thus also he calls men out of darkness into his light. We are called into a new life that previously was not there. We are called into the new creative possibilities of God in order to be free in them. It is important for us to adhere to this call. It is not the feeling which we receive thereby, and not the change of life which we experience, but only the call itself that guarantees the freedom to which it calls. Even if the feeling of freedom disappears, even if the individual life is disappointed, this call remains: you are called to freedom.

Further: by what, however, are we called to freedom? Does the call still sound like a command? Then it must now be evident that the language of liberation, in truth, is the language of love. Through love we become free. Many think they would then be free if they were so independent that they need ask no one for anything nor thank anyone. But that idea is superficial and often conceals the most bitter loneliness. We must maintain our self-sufficiency against foreign authority, it is clear. But we first become free when we perceive a love which does not dictate and does not command, which accepts us and gives us courage for ourselves and our new possibilities.

The call to freedom of which Paul speaks here stems from the pain of God and the love of Christ on the cross. In his cross God is with man—indeed, nearer than we think. Here he is not the superauthority in heaven that makes men into slaves of its law. Here God is nothing other than the secret of the dying love of Christ which awakens us to freedom.

In the torment of the forsaken Christ, the Father takes on the pain of man's self-indebted servitude. God gives himself in order to become the forsaken God. That is the secret of this freedom: wounds are healed through wounds, sickness is healed through sickness, and through the self-degradation of God men are made free of their servitude. "He divested himself, accepted the form of a servant, degraded himself even to the death of the cross," Paul says in Philippians 2:8. Liberation thus originates out of the sorrow of love for those in bondage.

Against a satisfied or indifferent heavenly power, we can and must rebel. But in this conflict it is not a matter of freedom, but only of power. Against direct love, we can remain aloof while we despise it. But against the pain of God, whose basis of love is in the Crucified, we cannot hold out, for it places us in the freedom of a life which is loved with pain and it also remains true to the godless. The more we grasp this pain of God, the more we perceive its disarming freedom. The nearer this love of Christ is brought to us, the more we are able to breathe freely.

The basis of the real freedom of man lies in the pain of God in the love of Christ. We run after false gods when, in our noisy anxiety, we betray this freedom in the religious and moral law, or only do out of sheer arrogance what pleases us.

Finally, from what does this love liberate us? In our context, normally it is said to be the "flesh." But, please, let us not think of the so-called fleshly sins, or of the freeing or renunciation of instincts. This expression has little to do with that. Rather flesh is the pressure always and everywhere to have to serve oneself. Flesh is the idolatry and the person cult in which we are concerned only with ourselves. Flesh is unfreedom. Flesh is being able to love no more. "Everyone loves only himself, but no one loves me," says the flesh in us. Everyone wants to be his own lord and everyone becomes

The Gospel of Liberation

thereby his own slave. We serve ourselves, honor ourselves, seek to affirm ourselves. Why? Because we have no self-trust, and we can have no self-trust because we know ourselves loved by no one. What remains other than to love oneself? Since one does not know who he is, he is then also full of desires and would like to find himself in the desired objects. They shall fulfill him, elevate him, and make him great. "I am what I can obtain." He is really somebody if he has income, house, car, pleasures, and obligations.

But then he is only what he has in himself—nothing.

In love, we can laugh about that because we have found ourselves, and we are free of this desire of having and of self-affirmation. The unfree man is the fleshly man. The fleshly man is the unloved man. The unloved man is the godless man, because he makes himself into his god. And because no one can play God well enough for himself alone, he usually needs his fellow man in order to degrade him and to be in the right. He particularly needs those who are foreign to him: Jews, blacks, foreign workers, long-haired youths, or the evil bourgeoisie. As self-styled, fearful mini-idols, man becomes in fact "the wolf of man," and not only in private, but also politically and socially.

Genuine freedom is born out of true love, if it is also true that a genuinely free life is a life in love. We will investigate in the areas of personal life, the life of the church, and society.

In personal life, whoever is liberated must watch that he does not relapse again. Freedom does not make life easier. It is much simpler to let ourselves be propelled and moved than to stand in freedom and to take life into our own hands. Paul therefore warns the liberated: "Do not use your freedom as an opportunity for the flesh," that is, give the flesh no "favorable opportunity" again to rule over you.

Long ago, men understood this as a call to asceticism and self-rule. They began to kill their flesh, attempting to bring their desires under control. They began to fight with their higher moral ego against their flesh, which, like an animal, lies in ambush in their human desires and impulses. They began to fight and devour and lacerate themselves. "Making war upon yourself is the most difficult war; conquering yourself is the most beautiful victory," they said to their children. Hold yourself under control, be lord over your own feelings, chastise your drives through renunciation! Deny and renounce yourself!

To be sure, this kind of self-dominated living standard is not written about very much today, where everyone is constantly pressured to pleasure through advertising. But there are still great examples and prototypes of this asceticism. Their sorrow lies in that man is so alone and lonely here. He controls himself, he rules himself, he tears himself to pieces, lacerates himself. He becomes his own wolf. But we cannot thus contain freedom nor remain firm in it. Paul has a much simpler solution—give the flesh no further opportunity, but through love, serve one another.

Self-love disappears and its opposite, self-hate, is entirely superfluous where we no longer serve ourselves but love another and serve him. Where we experience love, we are free, and we remain free where we begin to love. The relationships within us then rule, for when we go out from ourselves in love we are at one with ourselves; the anxiety we feel before our desires and feelings gives way to a new spontaneity.

What, however, does love bring to the other person? It participates in his burden and lightens the load he has to carry. And love expects for the other that freedom which we ourselves have experienced. Love liberates from loneliness, from anxiety for one's own life. It recognizes the other so that he no longer has to fight for his acknowledgment. Creative in its innermost energy, it brings into the life of another something new.

It can turn into love of the enemy. It destroys the madness of that friend/enemy-thinking, of self-assertion. It would like to be one with the other who is different from oneself, and one with the enemy who is disputing the individual right—the joy—to rejoice mutually in freedom. In summary, freedom is not that independence which finds its boundaries only at the autonomy of a neighbor. Freedom is actual and concrete only in the community of love, of mutual service, of mutual recognition, and of the joy in one another. Without community there is no freedom!

What then does this mean in the life of the church?

The Christian church is basically the brotherhood of the liberated. It extends in truth so far as it extends freeing love. The reality of our churches and communities, however, does not always agree about that. "The time of biting and of tearing each other apart between Catholics and Protestants fortunately is past," one sees in the announcement of a worship service in the newspaper. Still, the position of reciprocal eradication has not yet been replaced by the passion of a common love, but only a kind of liberal tolerance. We are still anxiously guarding our own possessions instead of rejoicing in those of others. Even so, the ecumenical spirit has today inundated the beaches of ecclesiastical institutions. An ecumenical solidarity in common political and social actions, in common worship, and also in the common eucharist has broken out in spontaneous groups in many countries. Nevertheless, institutions and church laws remain provincial, and many of their pious representatives consider such uncontrolled movements with mistrust, even attempting to hinder them. Thus Lenin's sentence, "Trust is good, but control is better," continues to hold sway and blocks freedom in love.

Many progressive Christians feel themselves more in limited community with the progressive Christians in another situation than with the conservative confederates in their own church. Two years ago, they closed the first common Protestant-Catholic *Kirchentag* in Frankfurt; in the discussions afterwards, many ecumenically active groups and theologians of both sides were shut out. Now only a timid "Ecumenical Pentecost meeting" in Augsburg remains—as if one could hold the spirit of Pentecost under control. Mistrust between confessions has become less, thanks be to God. But now a new mistrust between conservatives and progressives, between movements for the "Bible and confession" or for "Pope and church" on the one hand, and the so-called modern critical socially-engaged groups on the other is beginning to erupt. The sad spectacle of "biting, devouring, and tearing each other to bits" has transferred itself only to another front.

When will Christians finally cease this cannibalism? Preaching toleration can help, but it does not do it. Only the remembrance of the pain of God and the love of the Crucified can drive anxiety from our midst and establish hope upon freedom in community. Active ecumenical groups everywhere must infiltrate the institutions of anxiety in our churches, overcome them, and make them superfluous. Ecumenism is the cause of the whole people of God, not only the affair of ecclesiastical representatives. Ecumenism grows from underneath out of the spirit of free community with Christ.

What does that mean in society?

That the man of men wants to be God, and in practice becomes the wolf of man but cannot be the man of men, is a universal social and political fact. We live in a divided world. Racism, class warfare, power struggles, riches, and poverty mark the face of the earth, which has yet seldom seen the humane man. The sarcastic remarks of Paul—"But if you devour one another, take heed that you are not consumed by one another" (Gal. 5:15, RSV)—we take as an apocalyptic formula today.

To be sure, we know no separation of races here (in our

congregation) since we are not a racially mixed society. And still, we live in a segregationist society. Freedom and living space are there for the clever and for those who have arrived. But where is freedom for the children on our streets, for the aged, the handicapped and the injured? The old in our rest homes, the sick in our hospitals, the prisoners in our jails, the handicapped in our institutions—the rest belongs to them and they can divide the booty among themselves. The more men, the more generations that must live together today, the stronger becomes the public push to segregation, to separation. That is also a laceration, not through devouring, but through organized displacement.

The community of the free extends as far as love extends to the person who is different and to the foreigner. This community of Christ reaches beyond the union of churches and prevails in the traffic of our society wherever strangers and foreigners and enemies are shown love and offered freedom. The true community of Christ consists not only of the believing who can love, but also of all the displaced who hunger after recognition. "Whoever hears you, hears me" still stands as the apostleship of every Christian. "Whoever visits the captive, the handicapped, the oppressed, the neglected, visits me" shows the way into the hidden brotherhood of Christ in our society. Here an entirely different ecumenicity is still waiting on Christendom. Here the bitten and devoured ones are waiting on the appearance of the humane man who will save them and who will silence the biting and despising ones. Ecumenism is not only an internal Christian affair between separated churches, but also the common responsibility of love and the liberation of man from inhumanity in our society. It is certainly not wrong to discuss the Lord's Supper in order to come to a common conception. But still more pressing, it appears to me, is to break bread in common with the hungering, the old, and with strangers, and to celebrate this community because one first finds their joy in freedom.

Men are called to freedom through the pain of God in the love of the Crucified.

A free life is a life in love in community with others from whom men have separated themselves.

Freedom can make one anxious. But anxiety is not in love. Love overthrows in practice the law with which one suppresses or wants to pretend freedom. What would it be like if just once the time were to come when one did not receive negative answers to the question what is a Christian; that is, that he is one that does not do this or that, but instead, a positive answer, that he is a free lord of all things, and under no one, and is at the same time a free slave of all things and open to everyone?!

What would it be like if the time were to come when men would say, as they did about the Christians in old Rome, that they feed not only their poor but the entire city?

What would it be like if an ecumenical Christendom were to enter into the community of the damned of this earth? It would become then a symbol and sacrament of hope on earth.

We are all called to this freedom.

6

Faith and Brotherhood

For in Christ Jesus you are all sons of God, through faith. For as many of you as were baptized into Christ have put on Christ. There is neither Jew nor Greek, there is neither slave nor free, there is neither male nor female; for you are all one in Christ Jesus. And if you are Christ's, then you are Abraham's offspring, heirs according to promise.

Galatians 3:26–29, RSV

Who am I actually? What does it mean to be a human being? We must all answer that fundamental and penetrating question in our life from day to day, in all our human relations and vocations. Often it is a question of life and death. Every thought, every deed, every encounter is an answer one way or another. As children we had games and contests, tests of courage and disputes in order to find out who was the strongest and with whom we could be friends. Later we select a vocation in order to show what we can do. We want to know who we are and to let others know. And if in the demands and responsibilities of the day we wear ourselves out and come home exhausted, then this question hangs over us again and we sigh: "I have lost myself. I don't know who I actually am at all. If I could only come to myself again." "Who am I?" is a question that accompanies us our whole life long and gives us no peace. Often it sounds like an enticing problem. Just as often it pecks like a vulture into our consciousness and pounds like an unknown fist on our neck.

There is something in this for all men. Man is hidden from himself. Dostoyevsky wrote, "The ant knows the formula of its ant hill, the bee knows the formula of its beehive. They know its formula not in a human way, but in their own way. But they do not need more. Only man does not know his formula." Dostoyevsky is right. We, in fact, do not know our formula, and therefore we search for it. To be a man is a risk, an adventure, a hope, and, at the same time, an anxiety for all other beings. One cannot tell whether man will come to good or to evil. Unrest proceeds from him and uncertainty surrounds him. He can lift himself and his neighbors to heaven on earth. But he can also make life into hell for himself. Who are we?

With his sermon, the apostle Paul opens before us two ways of life: the life of the slave and the life of the Son of God. What does he mean by that?

A man can attempt to establish his identity through great works. Who he is depends then on what he does for others and what others think of him. Thus he builds his monument. Therewith man stands under law. Every day he hears the command of his ambition: You must accomplish something respectable. You must prove to yourself and others that you are a good man, a clever worker, a nice comrade, or a lovely woman. You must find recognition so that you can hold yourself in esteem.

This voice of ambition is basically the voice of groundless

anxiety in us. Because anxiety gnaws at us, we seek recognition and affirmation. We misuse others in vocation and in love and in the family as the means for the purpose of our self-realization. If we find praise and affirmation, then our self is lifted. If we find criticism and neglect, then we fall into depression. We need the congenial group to carry us. Often, however, we also need the others—the Communists or the Establishment—in order to raise ourselves against the opponent.

This Pharisaism is typical for the life under the law. We want to be what we are not and do not want to be what we are. Paul designates all this as slavery under the law. If we live like this, we live as slaves of our anxiety and we spread anxiety around us. The glory of works is the symbol of slaves. They must make something out of themselves, because they are nothing in themselves; and this "nothing" frightens them to death. All of us, students and professors, haves and have-nots, men and women, are up to our necks in this anxiety which produces hate and vanity.

Paul, however, shows us the other way—the way into freedom. He announces to us the crucified Christ as the salvation from anxiety and the torment of law. Is it not as if he were to say: Be not dependent on your works nor in pride over the good, nor in depression over the bad. Look no longer to yourself. Look beyond your own hand. Look to Christ who gave himself to you in death. In him you find yourself again, deeply loved in eternity. Strike out your ego— your sky-high exalting ego and your ego which casts you to death—and you will be happy, for in the Christ of God we recognize a divine love.

And where we always hear and experience the reality that we are loved, we become free from ourselves. The battle for recognition stops. The anxiety of coming off badly in life disappears. We can accept ourselves as we actually are because we are accepted by God in a love which does not seek its own. We can again have trust just as trust appeared to us in childhood. We are at home everywhere and can breathe freely because this love of God surrounds us on all sides like a cloak of freedom.

No one can earn this love himself. Finally, also, no one is a son of his parents through good works. Only out of the love of his parents is he born and is he what he is. Actual freedom and that trust which is better than all control comes always out of free unearned love.

"You are all sons of God through faith in Jesus Christ," proclaims Paul to the Galatians. I do not believe that they were better men than we. Paul did not see in them any reason at all to maintain such a thing. They were probably just as full of hope and just as doubtful, just as proud, and just as sad as we. Accordingly, they and we are sons of God through faith in Christ, since by this Christ God's unconditional love comes and finds them and us where we are always squatting. And this love changes us more radically than all learning processes. From unfortunate and proud idolators of anxiety it makes us into true men again, into children of the joy of God, into sons to whom the world stands open, and into heirs of the future where everything will be new.

Every fish needs water in order to swim. That is his element. Every bird needs air in order to fly. That is his element. And we men need trust in order to be able to live freely and humanly. That is our element. The boundless love of God which we recognize in the sorrow and death of Christ is like the atmosphere in which we are awakened to a free and human life. The glory of accomplishment and the society of accomplishment in which we live is the symbol and actuality of slavery. Trust and freedom, however, are the nobility of the sons of God.

This faith which is born to freedom out of trust is, however, only one side of the event of Christ. Paul indicates another point where man causes man to suffer. Wherever men come together, they soon begin to separate and divide themselves from one another. Israel distinguished herself from the heathen through the privilege of divine election. The Greeks considered themselves better than the barbarians on the basis of their culture, education, and wisdom. The lords separate possessions and goods from the poor. Men degrade women out of many well-known psychological reasons. We separate ourselves from other men through pride in our birth, our education, our position of well-being, our skin color, our religion, and God knows what else we will still find.

By nature we are inclined to gather together only with men who are exactly as we are, who think the same, who feel and believe as we do. Our societies are all-exclusive. Men like us affirm us. Strangers make us uncertain through being different. "Birds of a feather flock together." "There is honor among thieves." With these old proverbs, Aristotle had already shown in the *Nicomachean Ethics* that it is only sympathy, friendship, and brotherly love which gathers together the community of the like and the like-minded. But such societies are exclusive and therefore, at the same time, repressive toward the so-called "different ones."

Such societies today set in motion *apartheid* politics, persecution of Communists, Democratic hunts, persecution of Christians, anti-Semitism, racial hate, and so on. The more we grow together today into one world, the more men of different types mix together, the more dangerous will this be considered by society. The earlier, often only naïve, exclusivity produces today the emotional schemata of hate, friend/enemy-thinking, and apocalyptic terrorism which pushes toward "the last battle." The revolutionary movements of our time unfortunately are all too often just like the embattled establishment. The "being different" of the other is no longer endured. The enemy is no longer a man and must be liquidated. I believe that problem, again, is rooted in the enormous and overpowering anxiety which is an inevitable by-product of arrogance or hate.

But when the love of God liberates us from anxiety's hellish power, *that* has consequences for the changing of this exclusive and repressive society in which we live. The justification by grace only, by faith only, which we experience in Christ as the birth of our freedom, becomes transformed into the social power of the "justification of the other." For that love, the love in Christ who died for his enemy and for us when we were enemies, is not sympathy with those like us and not brotherly love for friends, but *agape,* love for others, presuppositionless love, love for enemies. Jesus did not hobnob with those like himself, but with those unlike him—the different, the ones shut out from society. That brought him to the cross. But that means God loves the godless. He justifies the sinner; he redeems the enemy and always just them. His love is not like ours, drawn to people like ourselves, the pretty, and those who affirm us. Rather it is a creative love which makes the hateful beautiful, brings the false into truth, and transforms evil into good. Such creative love is the true reality of the Christian church and can become its power in this world.

What is the Christian community other than the social reality of the "justification of the different," his acceptance and recognition as man? The church is indeed no religious or dogmatic community of Christians who all think and feel the same, but the concrete overturning of exclusive and repressive societies at their boundaries. Then only can this community break down and destroy the fences built between men, by anxiety and contempt. In this creative community there is no more Jew and heathen, Greek and barbarian, lord and slave, man and woman, black and white. They are all one in Christ. One becomes to the other as Christ, as the liberator out of his limits and boundaries. Christian community does not mean for me to sit next to someone with whom I am in agreement, but next to one with whom I am not in agreement.

A wave of freedom went through the ancient world when men gave up their prejudices, when they lost their nations, races, classes, and idols, and found in the universal church the new humanity. They were called the new people of God and the third race.

A movement of peace, the truce of God went through the feudal world of the Middle Ages when men forgot their vendettas and found reconciliation at the table of the Crucified.

On just such fronts can we today also find the creative reality of love, of the justification of others, and of the church. Where we respect in the opponent the image of God, where we recognize in the enemy one who is loved as we, where despising is replaced through recognition, and control through trust, there originates true community in Christ. We need a basic reform of our church structure in order to break out from the specter of party divisions, denominations, special interests and herd instincts, and to redeem the promises of the open church.

Then the Christian community will be the reality of the justification of the different in this world and an avantgarde of the coming world of the Son of Man. To be sure, what we can realize of this creative justification of love in our lives are always only fragments and small steps. But it is up to the vision of the Christian hope to see in those fragments the form of the coming whole, and in the earthen vessels of Christ's church the beauty of his coming kingdom of peace. What is realized in the productive justification of the different through Christ is always human and mostly all too human, yet I firmly believe that this is where the sacrament of hope is actualized for the future of the human race.

Through the cross of his Christ God offers us his open hand in order to transform us from slaves of anxiety into free sons of trust. And from all countries and peoples others stretch out their hands in order to find in us the free men of God.

Do not let these hands be empty. Grasp these open hands

and hold them firmly. That is the offer of life. And in the new community with God and with others we will experience who we actually are:

We are sons of God in faith.

We are all one in Christ Jesus.

We will live in peace and overthrow the power of anxiety.

7

LOVE AND SORROW

We rejoice in our hope of sharing the glory of God. More than
that, we rejoice in our sufferings, knowing that suffering produces
endurance, and endurance produces character, and character produces hope, and hope does not disappoint us, because God's love
has been poured into our hearts . . .

Romans 5:2b–5a, RSV

These are the words of a man from the early period of
Christendom when Christianity was still something of a small
radical minority. These early Christians had an experience
which made them break completely with old society. Different from others, they were strangers in their own families,
their cities, and countries, and they both attracted and repelled
other men. For they practiced a revolution of love and of
hope in a world where thousands of idols and demons and
numerous cults had to guarantee and embellish the existing
goods. They felt themselves free from all these idols which
had to be served in order to achieve a feeling of well-being.

They felt themselves free from the religious law of Israel and its permanent pressure of performing good works. And they knew themselves subject to no one any longer in the absolute sense, not even to the Roman god-emperor. Only the birth of their freedom out of the crucified Christ was obligatory for them.

Today Paul's words about hope, sorrow, and love still sound beautiful in our ears. But they have become church language which corresponds little longer to the practice of life. Let us make a check list.

Do we actually extol the hope for a future splendor which God will give? If we are honest, whether Christian or not Christian, then we will admit that such hope is still far too high for us to grasp. Naturally, the future oppresses us. We do not know what is going to happen. Naturally, we are anxious about it. What will become of our children? The world changes quickly. Will they succeed? What will come of the world which we have built up? We crouch under the atomic clock of war. The tensions of the cold war have become sharper. Men are still dying senselessly in Viet Nam. In Biafra, millions starve. A humanity which commits suicide to seeing eyes is a horrible vision.

We not only have cares for the future, but an indefinite fear and a general anxiety in the face of it. Whatever the future may bring, we certainly do not glorify it. Instead, we glorify the present which we possess and want to enjoy. Let us eat and drink, for tomorrow we die is a realistic philosophy.

Only the poor live by the hope for the future—if they actually live. The rich, however, live by the pleasure of the present and will also defend it. Rich Christians and Europeans will make no exception of that.

Do we extol suffering and sorrow? Not honestly. To be healthy and integrated, a man must be capable of work and pleasure. We can glorify success and luck, but can we also glorify sorrow, pain, suffering, and sadness? No, they cannot be glorified, but only avoided. To be sure, many are down in the dumps, as we sometimes say, but they are not extolling suffering, only feeling sorry for themselves. We can perhaps endure sorrow, sickness, and sadness if we have a strong soul, but that unfortunately does not make a name for us. In our present-day society, on the contrary, we use every possible means to push aside the experience of pain and sickness, or of sadness in the case of death. We can no longer be sad since that does not serve life. The incapacity for sorrow and "the capacity for sadness" (Alexander Mitscherlich) are typical for our society and have become notorious in our attitude on life. Many simply do not know how they should conduct themselves in such cases. "The people in the city can no longer be sad," said one farm woman in my church, and she was right. We can see it ourselves, as we avoid such "cases" and push these dark thoughts from consciousness.

Where lies the basis for our hopelessness and our incapacity to suffer and to be sad?

In New York not long ago a man was overtaken in bright daylight on an inhabited street, knocked down, and robbed. People stood around and looked on as interestedly as if it were a criminal novel.

In Rome a suicide sat hours long on St. Peter's Dome. A thousand-headed group stood by and waited for the sensational to happen.

In the newspaper in the last week there was a caricature: two Christmas shoppers in fur coats passed by a youth with a little box who was collecting for Biafra. One shopper was saying: "I thought that everything in Biafra was already at an end."

If we do hear or experience something in ourselves, then we say spontaneously: there is no longer even any love among men. I believe that hits the nail on the head. Neither divine nor human love is in the hearts of those who, as they say themselves, take everything coolly. "The dark and the great cold" of which Bert Brecht spoke, is gaining ground in our society. Those are the costs of the society of well-being. The incapacity to love is growing rapidly, and "those are in darkness who cannot see" (Bert Brecht).

Where love grows cold and systematically is being super-cooled, hopes for the future grow pale on the horizon of our consciousness. Where love fails, we lose the capacity to suffer and to grieve. Where the power of love fails, however, for suffering and for sacrifice, the capacity for suffering with one another is destroyed also. We can no longer ignore the situation of that robbed man, of that suicide, and no longer ignore the starving of Biafra, or the burned-out ones in Viet Nam. We can no longer identify and speak jointly with them because we no longer want that. The readiness to feel another's suffering as one's own and to take it on oneself, and the power to overturn this misery with hope depends on the power of love. If we want to have something to do with a positive hope for the future and with the humanity of a unanimous love, then we must break practically with those conditions which surround us with resignation, with coldness, and with lovelessness; which do not let us be the men we should and would like to be.

How does one come to that?

A person who has never been loved gains the power for love only with great difficulty. But everything will be the same to the person whose love has been manifoldly disappointed. To be sure, we find love to be beautiful and right, but mostly it is unattainable for us. It goes beyond our powers. Paul does not start out from an ideal, but from a concrete example: the love of God which is poured out in our hearts, he calls it. What does he mean? Where has he found the source for this love which raises us beyond our limits? He has found it in the coming, in the sorrow, and in the death of Jesus. He has not found God in heaven, but has recognized in the Crucified One on this earth the actual God who has already sought him in love and in the sacrificial death of Christ, and who has already found him a long time ago. Paul, who also wanted to love, but could not, found, in the death of Jesus, a love which came to meet him.

Our capacity to love is always born out of the experience of being loved. This experience is deepest when someone sacrifices his time, his power, and in certain circumstances, also his life for us. A doctor sacrifices his health for his patients. A teacher wears herself out for her students. A mother often gives more than her life for her children. But whomever one loves thus must also be worthy of that love. The deepest love, however, would be that where someone stood up for another and gave his life for a being unworthy of love, for people who cannot hope, who cannot suffer, who cannot love.

Such a love Paul called the love of God. And this is the love Paul experienced in Christ, for He gave his life "when we were still sinners," "when we were still godless," "when we were still enemies," when we were still unloved—loveless. That love is beyond us men. We love what is beautiful. Our love is awakened by what we deem worthy of love. But divine love—love which is born of the cross, is a creative love for the unworthy, the hateful, the painful, and the downtrodden. It makes esteemed men of sinners, it makes open men of embittered ones, it makes loved ones of the loveless.

Such love is actually selfless love because it is submission without anxiety. Such love is actually the affair of God, and where it happens to us, it lifts us beyond ourselves. If we value ourselves correctly, then we actually need this love to be able to live and to be able to love on our part. For who are we? How worthy of love are we actually? To believe that someone has died for us out of love, that someone may suffer for us because he loves us; to believe and to know that someone is there who does not give up on us, to whom we are of unending value, someone who waits and hopes for us—that gives us an invincible place of security and freedom, and that is the beginning of everything.

The certainty of being loved without end changes life. Not only can life experiences be explained differently, but other life experiences become possible. We can extol suffering and self-denial because we have discovered a new sense in it.

Suffering brings patience, says Paul. Normally, suffering makes us impatient; our patience is no cable line of strength but only a fragile "thread of patience." If we should, however, be freed from anxiety and greed of life, does there not lie then in patience something of the most deeply positive and human, namely, the power to accept something unbearable and to remain in love?

Patience brings experience, says Paul. Exactly translated, that means that patience brings confirmation, steadfastness. That, too, is normally not the case: patience more often tires and exhausts us. That one accepts sorrow in patience, conquers and remains in it in face of the abyss of embitterment, is like a miracle. It is grace.

Confirmation finally brings hope, says Paul. And that also is somewhat new, for normally our hopes end in our sorrow. A hope which is engendered in sorrow through patience and proof is a vital power which should not fear death, as do all the other hopes we have. It is a hope which does not let us come to nothing if a life's work shatters and we destroy ourselves. I remind myself often that this hope must be the power of the temporal and eternal life in that in our mortal nature it is the echo of that love of God which is stronger than death.

God hopes in us if he loves us. Therefore, let us not permit this hope to come to nothing. "We are afflicted in every way," says Paul, "but not crushed; perplexed, but not driven to despair; . . . struck down, but not destroyed; always carrying in the body the death of Jesus, so that the life of Jesus may also be manifested in our bodies" (2 Cor. 4:8–10). Thus can the experience of sorrow and patience in sorrow lead always deeper into the security of divine love and teach us the true power of hope. Then we can in fact extol the school of sorrow and self-denial and learn from those who have proved themselves in it, for they have grasped more the humanity of God than the successful, healthy, and fortunate who do not know darkness.

We come back to the beginning: a world without hope is a humanity which founders in care and anxiety and brings on itself those dangers which it fears. We stand today at the point where we gamble away the future of humanity because we give ourselves into the greedy pleasure of the present.

A world without hope is a humanity which has become incapable of sympathy and sadness. It is a world in which humanity and love become cold. Where men in this world recognize that unending and nondisappointing love which God brings over to them in the crucified Christ they become free and break with the system of coldness and of lovelessness. There the suffering of others becomes more important than their own pleasure in life. There hope becomes greater than the existing apathy.

Certainly, it is absurd for the hope of a future glory to extol itself in a society of well-being. Certainly, it is absurd to extol suffering in the circle of the successful and the healthy. Certainly, it is absurd to love there where others view everything coolly. But in a world of darkness and of great coldness, this hope, this capability of suffering, and this love is the one meaningful thing. It is a humanity which is covered by nothing other than by God. Whoever risks a life in hope, a life in love, trusts in God and is free from human fear.

*This message was presented
by Dr. Moltmann to the
General Assembly of the
Reformed World Confederation
in Nairobi, 1970*

8

Liberation through Reconciliation

That is, God was in Christ reconciling the world to himself, not counting their trespasses against them, and entrusting to us the message of reconciliation. So we are ambassadors for Christ, God making his appeal through us. We beseech you on behalf of Christ, be reconciled to God.

2 Corinthians 5:19–20, RSV

Therefore, if any one is in Christ, he is a new creation; the old has passed away, behold, the new has come.

2 Corinthians 5:17, RSV

With these unforgettable words, the Apostle Paul brings together the sum of the Christian message from God, the basis of faith and the practice of new life.

This is God, who in Jesus Christ takes the path to the cross, who takes suffering upon himself in order to reconcile the world. He dies the death of deepest forsakenness in order

78

to give his love to the world. He becomes poor in order to make many rich.

That is the world in which we live, suffer, and struggle—the creation which is not cast off, which is reconciled, loved, and not forsaken by God in the cross of Christ. It is not accused, but acquitted. It shall live and not perish.

And thus are we—in communion with Christ, a new creation free from the law of the old, perishing world, free from anxiety before its lords and powers, free from sin and death, and now open for the new life in joy, open for the salvation of the entire waiting creation, open for the coming creative affairs of God.

"Look, everything has become new. Look to the dying Christ and you see the dawn of the coming day of God who will transform everything!"

That is our lesson—to invite all men to the place of the poor, suffering, and dying Christ for reconciliation with God, to their new future, to freedom, to peace, and to righteousness. His cross is the symbol of hope for this earth. The reconciliation of God is the eternal living source of liberation for guilt-laden and dying men, for the degraded and wronged, for the poor and suffering.

Whoever believes in the God of reconciliation begins to suffer in this unredeemed world. He can no longer put up with the circumstances in the separated churches, in the divided world, and the inhuman society. He has become different. The world must not remain as it is. It is open for its freedom—its redemption—because it is reconciled in Christ. We hope for the future transformation of the world because we believe in the reconciliation of God.

Whoever believes in reconciliation begins to suffer in the church. The word *reconciliation* has been misused and betrayed by historical Christendom itself. False prophets speak of peace and call to peace where there is no peace. They comfort the people in their misfortune, telling them it is not at all so bad (Jer. 8:11). Appeasement is substituted for reconciliation, and religion is misused for the purpose of keeping the poor quiet so that the sufferers will be satisfied with unrighteousness and not protest it strongly. Faith is thus made to inhibit desire and deaden emotional states. The striving parties are called to reconciliation, to stay neutral and not take up sides. When we long for reconciliation with our enemies to whom we do wrong, we avoid therewith the confession of our own guilt. We exchange love with toleration over against evil.

Can one believe the churches, which preach reconciliation to others but do not themselves practice it so concretely as Jesus did when he healed the sick, cast out demons, and sat at the table with sinners and tax collectors? Why do many Christians turn away from the church and finally join social-revolutionary movements or new messianic cults? They see the churches and parishes to be more reconciled with the privileged of society and the good opinion of the powerful than with the crucified one. For this reason, the rebels hate the word of reconciliation, for they see everywhere the untruthful practice of "appeasement," which does not live and act "in the place of Christ," but is concerned for one's own salvation.

Reconciliation means new community with God and one another. How shall this new community be testified to credibly by the divided church? The separation of Christendom into various churches, their grudging concurrence in missions, the mutual discrimination of Christians through the laws of different churches is a scandal. It is a scandal not only before the world which sees this sad drama, but much more still a shameful scandal before the sorrow of the dying Christ.

If the churches of society today want to give something of Christendom, that is, of reconciliation, then they must let themselves be renewed. Whoever believes is in the first place Christ's, and only in the second place a member of "his" church. His suffering in "his" church springs out of his love for Christ who has loved him together with the world. Does this love for Christ and for the world lead forth today from among the established churches?

In many churches today, we find, to be sure, youth movements not only for a social-revolutionary transformation of the world, but also for the sake of Christ. These youth no longer find Christ in the church; they find him in the slums.

The church which has been separated for centuries finds itself today on the way—as we hope—to an ecumenical community. Modern social-revolutionary criticism of the churches, whether they are now separated or united, places us before new fronts in Christendom such as we have never before known but will be becoming ever more familiar with in the future.

In this situation, we should not shun suffering in the church in the love of Christ for the world, either through a conservative flight backward or a modernistic flight forward. Accepting that suffering, we may productively ask from it a new, credible community of Christ. Then, through God's reconciliation, can the churches be free again from their neglect and their downfall to the powers of this world. That is our hope for the church of Christ. We believe in the one church of God, liberated through reconciliation.

Whoever believes in reconciliation begins to suffer for the divided world. We have had to bury many hopes which were set on the humanization of the world by science, technology, rational business, and world politics. We live in a divided and alienated world. One division follows upon another, while, in a paradoxical way, the world grows ever more together into "one world." The Second World War left behind the East-West conflict, leading to the earth's division into the spheres of influence of the two white superpowers—Russia and America. Over the last twenty years the economic conflict between the rich peoples of the north and the poor peoples of the southern hemisphere has increasingly entered into the foreground. To the ideological conflict between capitalism and socialism has been added the race conflict. Wherever today are found race conflicts, ideological differences, social, religious, and national tensions, political peace will not be brought about through reconciliation; rather, there will be division, expulsion, dissension, apartheid, and ghettos. In Berlin an ideological wall was built. In Belfast there is a religious barbed wire fence. In South Africa and North America the making of ghettos continues. Whole populations in the Near East, in India, in Indochina have been expulsed and persecuted so that the different are among themselves. Divided cities, divided countries, separated men, castes and class systems mark the face of this earth on which men apparently can and want to live in a nonhuman way with other men. The motto of all conquerors who disseminate unfreedom is "divide and conquer," "rule through division." The life of mankind is oppressed by division and lordship. In this divided world, appeasement is no means of reconciliation, only a means to survive while one separates the strugglers and postpones their mutual annihilation.

Whoever believes in reconciliation begins to suffer at the inhumanity of man and his society. Wherever man leaves his humanity and makes for himself proud and doubtful gods of himself and his neighbors, he is inhuman, he has anxiety before himself and his neighbors. He can no longer love. And, loving only himself, he misuses his experiences, his possessions, and his neighbors for his own self-righteousness. They all must constantly say to him who he actually is and must appease his inner uncertainty. In his anxiety he depends on transitory things that must support his self-confidence. He expects from the good things of creation what only the creator himself can give him. He changes the splendor of the invisible God into an image just like transitory man (Rom.

1:23). He changes the truth of God into a lie and serves creation more than the creator (Rom. 1:25).

"The heart of man is an idol factory," said Calvin correctly. That shows up ahead of everything in the religion of man, which is always a "religion of anxiety." In this sense, man is indestructibly religious. His world is full of idols, gods, fetishes, and person cults—even his modern world. However, if man's heart depends on such idolized values and realities, then he is no longer free to accept the reality of his life without illusion and resignation, nor the different life style of anyone else. Every attack on his idols becomes an attack on his better self, and he reacts to it with murderous aggression. As such an idolater, man is in fact a neurotic being. Human societies which through political religions have lifted idolatry to the level of a cult are inhuman. Men are brought to sacrifice to the moloch of one's own proud nation. Humanity is brought to sacrifice to the fetishism of goods and consumption. While man has anxiety for the loss of his own pride he is not ready for peace. The idol factory runs full course in our nations.

Christ or these idols—that is the question. Whoever experiences liberation from anxiety by faith in the Crucified begins to suffer in the inhuman pressure of this anxiety. Whoever follows after the person who is crucified by the idols and powers of this world becomes ready also to be an iconoclast of freedom against those gods and cults of his society.

To demonstrate and to practice human liberation through God's reconciliation in this time means to preserve the long breath of hope between hate and rage, between reaction and revolution. We should consciously accept the sorrow of this time, making the cry for freedom out of the depth of the oppressed nations and men to be our own sighs and groans and answering with a call to reconciliation. The world can be made free through reconciliation. That is our hope for divided humanity—a humanity tormented by the idols of its anxiety. We believe in the one new humanity of God which is liberated through reconciliation.

Yet what is reconciliation? How does God reconcile in such a way that our ideals and our anxious dreams are broken and our divided and enslaved world changes and becomes free? Where is the reconciling God at work?

Whichever way Christian faith and theology today would like to go, Christ alone is our reconciler and our liberator. Whoever wants to know what reconciliation actually is must look to the path of Jesus. Jesus made the reconciliation of God real with the godless by healing the sick, driving out demons, fraternizing with lepers, sinners, and tax collectors, by championing the poor and oppressed. He lived and knew God's reconciliation in the midst of the conflicts of his divided society. The way of the Crucified became the way to the cross. In the loneliness of his death the reconciliation and the liberation of the entire godless world took place through the love of the Father.

What differentiates Christian faith from other religions and revolutions is the lordship of the Crucified. His cross separates faith from unfaith just as much as from superstition. What Christians believe and do must always be manifest and made righteous before the face of the Crucified. For through his suffering and death God once for all reconciled the forsaken world with himself, accepted it, and disclosed its freedom. Jesus did not reconcile God, but God himself reconciled the world with himself through the death of Jesus.

The cross of Christ makes public the cost of reconciliation (John 3:16).

The resurrection of the Crucified opens the universal future to the freedom it originated.

Let us make the cost of reconciliation clear. God did not liberate Israel out of slavery in Egypt through reconciliation with the pharaoh, but by the rescue of the persecuted and the defeat of the persecutor at the Red Sea (Exod. 14). According to Isaiah's vision of the future, for the salvation of his people out of the Babylonian exile this God will bring a great and distant people to sacrifice (Isa. 43:1–7). According to the gospel of the "new covenant," however, in the suffering and the death of Christ God brings his own son, that is, God himself, to sacrifice in love for the freedom of the world. In other words, the destruction and judgment have become so great, so world-wide, that God himself gets up and bears the sins of the world. Forsaken by God and men, Jesus dies lonely on the cross, thus taking on himself the loneliness and forsakenness and the burden of destruction for the entire world. That act creates freedom, peace, and a new joy for this world and all men in their life. This reconciliation is not simply maintained. It is no law.

This reconciliation comes into being through the representative suffering of Christ and the sacrifice of love. God did not look after himself, but gave himself for the reconciliation of the world and its freedom.

Reconciliation is an expensive grace. While God took the corruption of the world on himself, he created for the world its new future in redemption. We must understand that in the very suffering and death of Christ, God creates something new. God is "for us," for us sinners. God is "with us," with us godless ones. Reconciliation with God is created only by God himself. He is the subject and we are the objects of reconciliation. Therefore, the representation of Christ also is exclusive, unique, and unrepeatable. The reconciliation of God is the basis and the power for reconciliation between men who are enemies. God is "for us"; therefore, we can and should be "with one another" and not against one another.

The word from the cross is the gospel of God, as Paul says. Whoever does not begin here to believe God, to live with him, and to thank him has not yet begun with Christendom. We call the uncertainly developing Christianity to God in that we call all to the cross of Christ.

Reconciliation means here, in fact, that guilt is forgiven.

We know very well that no man and no people can recognize and confess their own guilt because they would then lose all self-respect. Guilt, therefore, is mostly pushed aside. But guilt which is pushed aside works further and poisons the life of a man and an entire people with hate for others and anxiety for oneself. In the cross of Christ, however, the guilty are not called to account and penalized. They are drawn to love and liberated. Guilt must no longer be pushed aside, but can be accepted as guilt forgiven.

Reconciliation does not mean only the forgiveness of guilt, however, but also the liberation from the power of sin. For Paul, sin is not only a guilt which we have, but still more, a power which totally enslaves us. It is the godless bond of death which through anxiety wins power over men. Because of this anxiety, the inhuman in us makes idols in the hope of finding certainty in transitory things. Fertility becomes the idol of anxiety. The nation or a leader becomes the god of anxiety. Men who are different become the phantoms and the apparitions of anxiety.

Anyone who is anxious is controllable and can be extorted and exploited. Liberation from the power of sin is also, therefore, always liberation from anxiety, liberation from idols, liberation from hate for men who are different from ourselves. This liberation from the power of sin takes place through the power of reconciliation. We find it in the resurrection of the crucified Christ from the dead. In Romans 11:15 Paul has brought together these two ideas—the "reconciliation of the world" and "life out of death"—for in fact, in the resurrection of the Crucified for us the power of death has been taken. Whoever is grasped by the spirit of the resurrected, which is the spirit of freedom, has no more anxiety; he is the friend of God even though the world is at enmity with him. He laughs at the lords and powers of this world. The evil bond of his lordship is broken wherever the Crucified becomes the leader of life in freedom. Whoever has no fear is not governable. He can, to be sure, be shot dead; but "it is a wonderful thing if one suddenly has no more fear."

Where has this liberation through reconciliation happened? The proclamation of the reconciliation of God brought Jesus into a deadly conflict with the public powers of his time— with priests and politicians. He was expelled from their camp and died "outside the door" (Heb. 13:12) between other rejected ones. Reconciliation, then, is created not in a holy place, nor in a religious sphere, but in the midst of the world and, to be sure, in its deepest point at a shameful place for the lost. We should, therefore, not make a cult out of reconciliation, which, separated from the sorrow of the world, is celebrated in the stillness of the churches, but seek and receive the reconciliation of Christ there where he has suffered. "Let us go out, out of the camp and bear his humiliation," says Hebrews (13:13). Reconciliation is not a religious cult for the pious, but the justification of the godless and the love of God for his enemies in the midst of their world. We must not let liberation through reconciliation be cooped up in a religious ghetto. The power of resurrection wants to renew the entire world from the ground up.

If the cross of Christ did not stand in a holy place, but there "outside," then neither does reconciliation belong in the inner parts of personal piety of the heart. We cannot lock up reconciliation in the ghetto of our hearts. We must receive the reconciliation of Christ and his freedom of resurrection where he has suffered, and that means in the midst of the actual inhumanities of our society.

To whom is the reconciliation of God in Christ of value? Paul knows two horizons here: reconciliation is of value on one for us (2 Cor. 5:18) and on the other for the world (2 Cor. 5:19, Rom. 11:15, Col. 1:20, Eph. 2:16). These are not contradictions, for reconciliation is valid for us together with the entire enslaved creation and is intended for the world throughout our lives. The horizon of reconciliation is in fact not any more narrow than the breadth of the entire creation of God. His reconciliation reaches as far as the clouds go. If Christians keep reconciliation a secret for themselves and give to the rest of the world only their sympathy or their developmental help, they betray the cross. That is a "Christian caste" which shuts itself off from the rest of population. If all cannot be reconciled, we also are not actually reconciled. We should, therefore, break out of our churches and out of the anxious egoism of our nations and develop a new piety of solidarity with all the damned of this earth. "God was in Christ reconciling the world," and the churches are not yet already "the world," but in the best sense a small beginning of that reconciled world of God. Out of the tension between "us" as reconciled, and the "world" as reconciled by God, originates the mission of freedom, the engagement for peace, and the sortie for righteousness in the world. The floor burns under our feet when we recognize this tension.

Finally, we should not forget that the reconciliation of the world is created through the bodily death and resurrection of Christ. The salvation of the world is therefore not only the salvation of souls, but together with that, the salvation of the body. "The body belongs to the Lord and the Lord to the body," says Paul (1 Cor. 6:13). He does not speak of a precedence of the soul. After having sounded the salvation of the soul and the rescuing of individuals for so long, we Christians are today beginning to discover the materialistic bodily components of salvation which lie in the new creation. "All the ways of God end in corporeality" (Otinger). Man is subjected bodily to death, sicknesses, hunger, exploitation, and degradation by other men. Together with the entire waiting creation Christians long bodily for salvation from transitoriness (Rom. 8:23). The reconciliation of the world completed in Christ opens to this world the wide and encompassing horizon of salvation, or redemption, of the kingdom in which God dwells with man. Salvation in this encompassing sense means Shalom—a new creation of the whole man according to the body and the soul, a new creation of the whole humanity according to persons and relationships, a new creation of Heaven and earth, so that righteousness and peace finally join together on earth. This is called resurrection. The more earnestly we take the bodily suffering and death of Christ, the more all-encompassing will we understand the eschatological horizon of freedom to be which his resurrection opens.

How is the reconciliation of the world with God exhibited in the symbol of the cross? How can we correspond to it credibly in word and deed? We accept here what the Reformed World Assembly thought and said in its last conference in Frankfurt under the theme "Come Creator Spirit."

The reconciliation in the cross is preached, lived, and accomplished in this unredeemed world through the power of the spirit. It is attested to by sermon, by community, and by deeds of righteousness. I would like to point out that the cross of Christ is not only the affair of Christian witnesses, but also impresses its form on this world.

Because we do not venture to state loudly and clearly enough that judgment which is bound with Christ by the cross, the word of reconciliation has indeed become cheap and unreal. The "word of reconciliation," however, is for Paul the "word from the cross"; this cross, which is for some a power of God, for many, however, is nothing other than folly and scandal (1 Cor. 1:18).

Reconciliation really has nothing to do with an indifferent neutrality. Jesus Christ himself preached the gospel of the near kingdom of God to "the poor" and not to "the rich." He was a friend of sinners and lepers, and not of Pharisees. His mission was available to all men in that he became an intense partisan of the weak, the discriminated against, and the hopeless. Jesus grasped the entire human society, so to speak, at its lowest point with the despised ones. Throughout the Old Testament, in spite of the special covenant with the people Israel, there already occurs the deep recognition: you are a God of the needy, the refuge of the oppressed, the sustainer of the weak, the refuge of the forsaken, the savior of the doubting. Thus present and conducting himself, God "pushes the powerful from their thrones and lifts the lowly. He fills the hungry with good things and lets the rich go empty" (Luke 1:51–53). Just as all flesh should see "together" the splendor of the Lord, God lowers the mountains and raises the valleys.

If we grasp this partiality of God and of the gospel today, then we will also understand again the "revolutionary" character of the Bible. Only for the poor is the message a joyous message. For the rich and self-righteous, it is painful. The message of reconciliation is not the religious honesty of the good society, but the salt of the earth. And salt in the wounds of the earth burns, but it hinders decay. We must obtain again the sharpness of the gospel if we want to spread the freedom of the Crucified out into this chaotic world. "Woe be to us if we do not preach the gospel"—woe be to us if we do not preach the gospel, but the law.

In return "we are invited to the place of Christ," says Paul. The Crucified invites us through humanity to reconciliation with God. One who invites has no great power. His hands are open and extended invitingly. He forces no one and compels no man. His invitation grants freedom and time to the invited. His perseverance in offering always opens anew to them a reconciling and free future. Lords command, judges judge, party leaders proclaim. God, however, lets us be implored by the dying Christ. He is the liberating God in a world of slavery and rebellion.

Reconciliation is lived in Christian community. That is the second thing. But how does the cross show itself in the life of the reconciled? Human societies adapt themselves naturally in the likeness of their members. "Birds of a feather flock together," said Aristotle. The same class, the same race, the same nation, the same economic order, the same views, and the same morals unite us with men who are like us, who affirm us. Men who are different unsettle us. We naturally love friends and despise enemies. The law of life of a Christian community, however, is not just this homogeneity, but the "acceptance of the other" in his differentness. This acceptance and love joins the unlike. Christian community brings into focus the reconciliation of the enemy with God in a divided world then if it consists of "Jews and heathens, Greeks and barbarians, lords and slaves, men and women" (Gal. 3:28). The walls and fences of the ghettos which men erect against one another in order to maintain their own dignity are overturned and broken down by Christian community, for in the spirit of reconciliation, the Crucified himself steps between enemies and calls a new community into life (Eph. 2:14 ff.). Old enemies and also old friendships break down in the face of the new creation in Christ. Then the church actually becomes the reconciling body of Christ.

But our churches and parishes are not like this. The natural and thus so inhuman principle of sociability always seems to succeed so that only the like find themselves together and the different ones remain outside the door. National churches, racial churches, class churches, middle class churches, are in their practical life heathenish and heretical. Through them, not reconciliation but contempt is disseminated. Not until a Christian community consists of the unlike, of the educated and uneducated, of black and white, of the high and the low, will it come to be a witness of hope for the reconciled world of God. Such a community will have difficulty in the divided world. Its members will be considered traitors of the "most holy goods" of their respective society and class. They will be a community under the cross. But we wait for such a community, for only in it lies hope.

The service of reconciliation takes place, finally, in actual deeds of liberation. The reconciliation in the cross of Christ has in itself a world-changing impulse. The resurrection shows it to us. If the power of death is broken, then the power of fate is broken also. When the spirit of resurrection rules there is freedom—world-conquering freedom, and therefore also world-changing freedom. When, by virtue of reconciliation, guilt is forgiven and hostility is conquered, a new future opens for which it is worth living. Whoever is reconciled is also changed. If God has reconciled the world with himself, then all relationships in this world are changeable for the person who believes. Nothing must remain as it is. Everything can become new.

Reconciliation without a change of men and their relationships is a weak consolation. Christians should perceive that today. Change without reconciliation leads to terrorism. Revolutionaries should recognize that today. For not until there is reconciliation will the compulsion of the evil deed which bears continuous evil be broken. Not until there is reconciliation will the devilish circle of revenge be destroyed. Not until there is reconciliation will the law of retaliation be conquered. Creative new righteousness, creative peace and a freedom such as the world has not yet scarcely seen originates out of reconciliation and not out of law.

The scheme of the divided world has eaten very deeply into human thought and feeling. It is our own anxiety which has taught us to hate the opponent. The person who preaches hate always has anxiety. It is through the propaganda of the dominant that the notion of friend-enemy dichotomy is brought to us. But Christ is not against "the Communists"; he died for them. Christ is not against the "whites"; he died for them. That demands from us a new thinking and a new solidarity of love, for only love overturns anxiety. Love includes the opponent in its thoughts and affairs. It sees in him the reconciled and liberated friend of tomorrow. It does now what is pos-

92   THE GOSPEL OF LIBERATION

sible tomorrow for it sees the opponent in the hands of the dying Christ. Love has, therefore, a critical trust in the changeability of the enemy and a permanent mistrust against the justice of one's own position.

In social and political conflicts, Christians are "unreliable confederates" for both sides. They also fight against unjust lords, against racists, and against exploiters. But they are immune to the leading of hate and of terror. They do not let the law of fighting be prescribed by the enemy, but with their own methods fight the battle to free opponents of conflict from their hate-producing and power-wielding anxiety. They know that God's reconciliation surrounds the opponent also, and therefore that righteousness can only be reached by mutual transformation. They cannot be forced to enter into the devilish circle of power and counterpower, for they want to overthrow this demonic circle and not to support it.

Mao says: "We intend, therefore, that war be abolished. We want no war. One can, however, only abolish war through war; and if one wants no more guns, one must take arms in hand" (*Words*, Peking 1967, 76). His enemies are exactly of the same persuasion. However, that is no hopeful dialectic, but a very doubtful one indeed. We intend, instead, that war be done away with. We too want no war. War can, however, only be done away with through creative peace. If we want arms no longer to be in hand, then we must fight for peace with the means of peace and make plowshares out of swords.

To be sure, it can be that Christians also doubt the removal of scientific and political unrighteousness with peaceful means and accept the recourse to power as the last resort. But they cannot justify the use of power, for then they assume guilt which must be forgiven. However, the person who does nothing in order not to be guilty still carries the responsibility of obedience to God. Mostly, however, we do not stop to consider this last question. Mostly, men are called to weapons because nothing better occurs to them in their anxiety. The person on whom this anxiety is no longer imposed should develop productive dreams for peace. We have invested rich scientific, technical, and strategic dreams in military death, but in life, in peace, powerless resistance, and the change of the opponent, on the other hand, almost no dreams.

Men who fight against each other, who persecute and destroy others, are reconciled in Christ even though they still are not redeemed. Thanks be to God. We and our enemies can be changed. The world itself has become a changeable world. God has made the impossible appear to be possible. Let us therefore already do today what shall be tomorrow. "The night is past, the day is coming near, let us finally do what we should" (Rom. 13:12), and grasp the freedom which reconciliation gives us.

9

The Peace of God

And the peace of God, which passes all understanding, will keep your hearts and your minds in Christ Jesus.

Philippians 4:7, RSV

"I came to cast fire upon the earth; and would that it were already kindled! I have a baptism to be baptized with; and how I am constrained until it is accomplished! Do you think that I have come to give peace on earth? No, I tell you, but rather division; . . .

Luke 12:49–51, RSV

Out of the depths we call to you, O Lord, and ask for peace. Forgive us our guilt which makes us peaceless and give us peace through grace. Take from us human fear and anxiety of death and give us peace through freedom.

Destroy the idols and the false securities on which our hearts depend and which deceive us day by day, and give us peace through faith. Be merciful to us and your entire waiting and groaning creation.

The bringing together of these contradictory words from the Bible is a montage. Perhaps one ought not actually to make something in this way. In this case, however, such a confrontation can call us from too dearly loved habits of thought and idleness.

"All speak today of peace—we, too," the statement often rings in our ears. We have talked about that for a long time already, almost from the beginning on. Every worship service for years has begun with the greeting of peace—peace be with you—and ends also with the wish of blessing—grant us peace. From Sunday to Sunday, from year to year, from century to century, the gospel of God is combined with all human wishes and hopes in one word, *shalom*—"peace."

But, if everyone speaks of peace and we also, that must indeed not be the same thing. What do we mean by peace? Whose peace do we mean? To whom do the benefits of peace come?

"Leave me in peace," says the person who wants to have his rest. "Have peace in the heart," says the other who does not concern himself for the evil world. "Peace to all men who are of good will"—but not to the others who are of evil will. "Peace to the houses—war to the palaces" demand others. "There is peace only on the other side of capitalism" —some say. "With Communists the only way one can relate is with weapons in hand," say others.

The more earnestly we hear all these voices, the more we recognize that it is not enough merely to praise peace, to extol readiness for peace, and to bless every speech of peace. There are too many false prophets who say: Peace, Peace! and there is no peace—even in the church. Peace is not always, nor in every case, good. Jesus did not come as a dear angel of peace who soothed and pacified the struggling. The manner in which he brought the peace of God to earth excited discord and division. In fact, he was crucified by the powerful lords of this world as disturber of the peace. To the apostles of peace of Christ no other fate was promised than sorrow, persecution, criticism, scandal. We must thus see exactly what "peace" is supposed to be, whose peace is meant, and to what extent peace is replaceable.

Peace, most people say, is the condition of life without power and threats of power, without oppression and aggression. Peace, furthermore, is an ordered life without conflict; thus, peace is mutual agreement, balance of power, harmony of different interests. They say finally, however, peace can also be established in necessary conflicts of various interests so long as the discussions are linked in peaceful, not belligerent or murderous paths. Then labor disputes can be regulated as affairs of social partners and structures can be created in which one can compare oneself with opponents.

Such orders of peace are powerful, but they are also constantly threatening orders. Between the world atomic powers, there is a peace of fear which rests on the balance of power of mutual capability of destruction. But this balance of power can easily be destroyed. Technocratic world peace can probably be produced only through a totally supervised world. But the dammed-up stuff of conflict will be frostbound like a battleship in mothballs in peacetime. The balance of power will be stabilized there, since every change in that respect which has come to the poor from the last war would throw the world back into that last war. Thus, for the continuing life of man, a world peace of this kind is perhaps "unavoidable," as C. F. von Weizsäcker said.

But the forebodings of those whose views these are as to what it will cost in adjustment and elimination of opposites are not particularly attractive. It must perhaps be thus because every alternative would blow the world sky high. However, that such a totally regimented world would be the fulfillment of all the desires and prayers for peace which move men, we scarcely want to accept. The absence of power seizures and coercive measures, of threats and aggression is certainly an inescapable condition for peace, but still actually not yet peace itself.

According to biblical terminology, peace, *shalom, eirene,* is much more than absence of war and absence of threats. Peace here is a positive word of salvation and means fortune, blessing, perfection, perfect joy, healing and well-being, freedom and righteousness, all in one; a condition, therefore, with nothing more to be wished for, a fullness of life which rejoices, laughs, jubilates, and dances in freedom from oppression and pressures in the present time of its creator. In such peace the present conflict would not be ordered but created as something new. It would, therefore, be called the "peace of God" because it would bring his entire creation into his joy and his fortune. This kind of peace is a new life and a new liveliness, not only the absence of threats of death and annihilation.

We need order; otherwise, chaos devours us, we say. God is also not a God of disorder, it says in the Bible; however, it does not follow that God would be a God of order. It does follow that God is a God of peace. His peace is not the same as painful, assiduous order which is wrested from chaos, but much more; namely, a life which is oriented in his godly fullness and no longer in the direction of threatening chaos. This peace can be called forth from a life of fulfillment, of God, through unpeace in the world, and can lead to conflicts, separations, and tensions. God's peace is directed in fact against chaos, but also against that power of ordering which has made a covenant with death and which also oppresses freedom and joy in life with the battle against chaos. This peace of God has nothing to do with the cries of peace of the "false prophets" who speak of peace where, in reality, there is no peace, but rule with organized peacelessness.

Jesus did not disseminate the peace of law and not the political peace of the Pax Romana, but an entirely different peace; namely, the peace of the God who is entirely other.

He glorified that blessed state which was rejected by the peace of the law and which received no place in the sun in the good society of the Pax Romana. The peace of God which he, in communion with sinners, the poor, and lepers, brought to the fore, worked publicly as a disturber of the peace in the ranks, and also in the conflicts of that world. As a denier of the idols of that world and as a disturber of the peace, he was expelled, cursed, and crucified.

If we speak as Christians of the "peace of God," then should we not consecrate every presentation of peace and speak "also" of peace, but remember, as radically as possible, that the peace of God the Father was represented, effected, and brought among us by the crucified Christ? Between the peace of God and the world stands the cross. The peace of God is thus a critical peace. Peace with God means, therefore, not gratification of the world and contentment in the world, but, throughout, also healthy discontent and unpeace with the powers and lords of this world. Is there then peace between the freedom of the gospel and the regulations of the law? Is there then peace between the new life and the alliance with death?

The peace of God is "higher" than all reason. It goes beyond all reason and is greater, Paul says here. This can be read to understand the problem that in all reasonable regulations on peace something is always lacking. Paul, however, was of the opinion that the peace of God was not only for the sake of God greater than human reason, but also that it was for the sake of the crucified Christ different from the peace of reason. Peace in the crucified Christ is a scandal to the Jews and folly to the Greeks. But Paul trusts thereon that the divine folly is wiser than men, and the divine weakness is stronger than men (1 Cor. 1:23-24), and he proclaimed the crucified as the power of the peace of God. That is in fact a foolish thing, to expect of that crucified, weak and poor Jesus a peace which is world-changing and which fulfills everything with salvation and life. How could a weak and poor God who was crushed under the wheels of power help?

There are many beautiful plans and programs with regard to the Christian contribution to world peace. However, which "contribution" do we actually expect from the Crucified on whom Christians still call? What does the Crucified contribute to the atomic, to the technocratic, to the religious and revolutionary world peace? Somehow he still contradicts our Christian expectation and activities also. Not only for the doubter—but also for the people who attempt faith—memory in him disturbs the circles one projects and in which one moves. We wish we could say it better: our Christian faith of peace is better than all peace of reason because the peace of God is even higher. And this too: by virtue of the Christian liberation of reason for itself alone, the Christian peace is the most reasonable of all rational peaces. The Crucified is different, and if he is "our peace," then that operates and transforms entirely differently. Which peace does God reveal through the Crucified?

We know the story in which the Scribes and Pharisees were pillorying a prostitute known in the city. She had offended against the law. The peace of law must be established. According to the law she must be stoned. "What do you say?" Jesus drew figures in the sand with his finger and was silent. They were importunate and would have liked to pin Jesus down. Astonished, he looked at them and said, "Whoever among you is without sin may seize the first stone and throw it at the woman." Then he painted further in the sand undisturbed. The accusers turned to one another. He said to the woman, "Has no one judged you? Then I do not judge you. Go and sin no more."

Now, unpeace originates through unrighteousness and punishment of evil testifies mostly to a new unrighteousness: "The others are guilty." Insofar as we punish them and call the guilty to account and liquidate them, we establish peace again. But, unconfessed guilt and the repressed past testify to aggressions. Our own guilt which we do not want to acknowledge we stick into our pocket and thus make the other into the sinner. Is that not a profound reason for the hate of foreigners, racial hate, anti-semitism, and so on? How should man who is without peace, who has disintegrated through guilt within himself, be able to create peace? Is then the beloved good here and the hated evil there? "Who among you is without sin?"

The peace which the Crucified reveals lies therefore in the forgiveness of sin, in the liberation from the power of guilt. Paul always says on that account, "grace and peace," thus peace through grace. That angers the moralists. Paul calls it "reconciliation." Peace through forgiveness of sin also grasps deeper than the moral. The man who is not liberated from guilt can also not live with the public guilt of his past. It oppresses and rules him unconsciously and makes him inhuman, and that not only personally but also socially. "We would also work for one dollar per hour if the Negro receives only fifty cents," said a white man in the southern United States. The aversion of many Germans to a reconciliation with the East malingers, to be sure, in the conception of a so-called unrenounceable position of law. But, does the basis not lie much deeper in the grumbling darkness of a collective unconscious which is defined by an evil past? The peace of God is created through grace.

Man always creates for himself symbols and values which become for him the basis of trust of his existence. Attacks on these symbols and values he feels therefore as attacks on his vital interests. Accordingly, he creates idols which should afford for him validity, affirmation, and certainty. I do not mean by that only the old and faraway heathen idols like Moloch or Baal, gods of fertility and gods of the states; but for us today the idolization of the living standard, of nation, of race, of progress, etc. If the rate of exchange of our idols goes down, if our social rank sinks, we become sour and become aggressive against foreigners, foreign workers, blacks, Russians, Jews, etc.

So long as man makes idols out of his life's environment, then his certainty of life is surrounded by anxiety. That makes him malicious toward others. So long as he prays to the idols, he is not able as a free man to affirm his life and at the same time the life of other men.

The freedom which is indebted to the faith in the Crucified One is a freedom from idols, powers, and lords of the world which brought Christ to the cross. In trusting the father of Jesus Christ, the faithful believer leaves idolized reality and becomes a free man who can both have and leave things. He becomes free to accept himself and at the same time to affirm the different life style of the other. He will laugh about small and politically puffed-up idols. They have no power over him. But that is very disagreeable for the unfree men who cling to their idols. He is for them a bird who dirties his own holy nest, or even a traitor of their most holy qualities. Nevertheless the destruction of hate and power begins with the liberation from fetishes, idols, and person cults which promise security and lead into death. Out of this, then, a conscious battle against such idolatries in our world of life should result. The work for peace must also be liberated from idols, for hate and power do not serve peace. The peace of God is given through liberation from idols.

Finally, out of the forgiveness of guilt and the leaving of the gods and idols originates freedom from anxiety and fear. "If anyone is in Christ, then he is a new creature. The old has passed away, everything has become new," extolled Paul. Still stronger, he says that whoever believes and receives his trust from the crucified Christ is already dead to the world of law and of death. He is also dead for the claims of law and of anxiety. And that in death also, moreover, the emperor has lost his law. Whoever no longer has fear can no longer be ruled. He can laugh at those who have been speculating at his anxiety. "It is wonderful when you suddenly no longer have any fear," said a black man from the Southern states. "We don't care if the whites show their arms and threaten to put them on." On June 17, 1953, for a short time in Berlin, the power of anxiety was broken because there were men who dug themselves in before the tanks. People spoke out freely in the streetcars. A similar freedom from fear was experienced in the Parisian May revolts of 1968.

Whoever no longer has fear can no longer be ruled, but he can be shot. This freedom is not cheap to have; therefore, freedom from human fear is always bound with freedom from anxiety of death. "Death is the actual counter-revolution," it said in 1968 on a Parisian wall. The Christian faith, which owes its freedom to the resurrection of the slain Christ, can point out well enough such cases of fearless resistance. For that we not only need to thank the martyrs of the Confessing Church, Paul Schneider and Dietrich Bonhoeffer. We can also practice the small, fearless events of daily life. Love makes considerate, but faith makes one fearless and does not let itself become entangled in open hesitation. Freedom from the anxiety of death and from the fear of man is the greatest gift of faith. Without such lived freedom, I see no meaningful peace coming.

Freedom from oppressing guilt, freedom from enslaving idols and gods, freedom from fear and anxiety—with these begin the peace of God who keeps our hearts and minds and our reason in Jesus Christ. That does not make logical rules of peace superfluous nor does it replace them. We have no patent key for all social problems, but we recognize in the Crucified a depth of peacelessness in the world and in ourselves through which we experience a freedom transcending all reason, indeed all expectations of reason. It is a special and characteristic front in which the peace of God is created through grace and freedom.

And what is the matter with social peace, with political and economic peace, with research of peace, and plans of peace? That belongs no longer in the sermon of an individual, but in the working circle and action groups of a church. It belongs in the common conversation of all who are perplexed over God's concrete will of peace. In conversation, we must hear and speak in order to come to common actions. Still, let us name here two perspectives which are, in general, appropriate:

1. "Further, dear brothers," says Paul, "what is true, what is honorable, what is right, what is loving, what is virtuous, what is praiseworthy; think on these things." Others can thus also know something, and we can learn something from all sciences and wisdoms in the world. The peace of God which comes to us in Christ and liberates through his cross does not shut us out from the world, as many believe and practice; but opens to us, in fact, the wider world and brings us into an educated solidarity with other men and into cooperation with them.

2. In spite of all the research and planning for peace, we should, however, ask the question "peace for whom?" We must act as counselors for men who have no peace, no life, no freedom. We should also become critics of those who mean by peace only their own peace, power and possessions.

May peace be with those whom we overlook, forget, or despise. Peace be with our enemies. Peace be with the Poles and the Russians and the Chinese. May peace be with the Vietnamese. May peace be with the Biafrans! May peace be with the aged, the forsaken, and the hopeless in our midst. May peace in grace and freedom be with us—and with them.

10

THE RETURN OF CHRIST

Jesus left the temple and was going away, when his disciples came to point out to him the buildings of the temple. But he answered them, "You see all these, do you not? Truly, I say to you, there will not be left here one stone upon another, that will not be thrown down."

As he sat on the Mount of Olives, the disciples came to him privately, saying, "Tell us, when will this be, and what will be the sign of your coming and of the close of the age?" And Jesus answered them, "Take heed that no one leads you astray. For many will come in my name, saying, 'I am the Christ,' and they will lead many astray. And you will hear of wars and rumors of wars; see that you are not alarmed; for this must take place, but the end is not yet. For nation will rise against nation, and kingdom against kingdom, and there will be famines and earthquakes in various places: all this is but the beginning of the sufferings.

"Then they will deliver you up to tribulation, and put you to death; and you will be hated by all nations for my name's sake. And then many will fall away, and betray one another, and hate one another. And many false prophets will arise and lead many astray. And because wickedness is multiplied, most men's love will grow cold. But he who endures to the end will be saved. And this gospel

of the kingdom will be preached throughout the whole world, as a
testimony to all nations; and then the end will come."

Matthew 24:1–14, RSV

Two things concern all of us daily: first, the future of
God, for we believe in hope and expect the fulfillment of all
our prayers. But at the same time also, we are concerned about
the future of the earth on which we live and work, love
and suffer with others. We know the war in Viet Nam. We
recognize the coming famine, and we would like to have
peace and righteousness on earth so that our children can
be happy, so that they will live with the children of all other
people in a human way. We read the Bible and we read the
newspaper every day. As we read the Bible, we would like
to participate in the promised history of God. As we read
the newspaper, we would like to be involved in the fate of
the world. But how can we bring both together: community
with hope in God and community with the sorrows of the
earth?

The first thing which springs before our eyes out of the
small Synoptic Apocalypse is the wide scope of questions
of the disciples. When will it happen, and what will be the
sign, they ask. But what should happen and why do they
look for a sign of assurance—of "your coming (parousia)
and the end of the world?" They ask about the setting up of
the kingdom of Christ. They ask about the end of a world
from need, tears, pain, and sin. They set both questions in
one. How can they do that? Now they have experienced
with Jesus the gracious nearness of the kingdom of God. The
passion of the hope of God has grasped them. Having left
everything, having become poor in the world in order to find
the kingdom of Jesus where the blind see, the lame walk,
lepers are made pure, and the poor hear the gospel, they
hunger for this future of Jesus. But they have also experienced with Jesus the boundless love for the forsaken,

despised, suffering creature, for sinners, tax collectors, and heathen. With him they have taken the sorrow of love on themselves. That is the sorrow of this time, sorrow which covers the entire world. Whoever loves begins to suffer; to him the suffering of the other is intolerable. Therefore, love hungers for the "end of the world," namely, for the end of need. Whoever enters into the community of Jesus always learns both emotions at the same time: the passion of hope that makes us joyful because the kingdom of God is near and the painful sorrow of love, experienced in solidarity with oppressed humanity. Because we learn both together with Jesus—hoping love and loving hope—we must, like the disciples, ask about the future which surrounds Christ and the world. His return, a completion of his kingdom, must be the end of all need in the world; indeed, it must call forth a new world. And on the other hand, the actual sorrow of man will only be conquered in the spirit and in the kingdom of Christ.

Granted, it is difficult for us today to bring the hopes of Christian faith and our sorrow for the fate of the earth into one common denominator. Many minds go their separate ways here: one believes in God but ignores the world as if it were nothing. The other involves itself politically and socially in the history of the earth and disregards God as if he were nothing. One considers faith in God and hope in Christ as an illusion. The other considers the quest for sense and purpose in world history as myth and speculation. The one overlooks the stimulus of world-conquering hope which Jesus brought into this world. The other does not see that the sorrow of love for this inequitable world is reality and not myth. Mere hope without love would be illusion. Mere love without hope would be resignation. True faith is alive in both.

When the disciples found the messianic hopes for heaven and earth fulfilled in Jesus, they were converted. From the ambiguous late Judaistic apocalyptic, they turned to Jesus and to a clear faith. Today men are not converted to the hopes of Christ if the Christians they see have not already been converted to the suffering of humanity.

But how should we live with this certainty of the future in history? What will happen to us? What should we do? The answer Jesus gave according to Matthew gives us a clear directive. His speech is so constructed that it goes from the external to the internal; it changes back and forth constantly between prophecy and admonition. Above the first part stands a great continuing "not yet"; if actually his kingdom ends this world time, then only he himself and nothing and no one besides is the "end of history and its solved puzzle."

Therefore, it means first: *do not let yourself be led astray*. There will be many who come and say: "I am the Christ, the leader, the liberator." They will say: "We bring to you the fulfillment of all desire. Whatever it is you Christians hope for only in God, we do. We bring the 'kingdom of freedom.' We build the kingdom of brotherhood and bring all need to an end. God is not yet helping you; leave him and join our movement. Save yourself. We will show you the way." No, it is not with evil that they will lead you all astray but, in the best of cases, with blessings. Even then, it is not their activity in the good but their faith that this is the end of the history of need that is misleading. Therefore they will urge you to call all your achievements very good, and in doing so to liberate your hopes. Your hope for Christ's Kingdom, where evil and death will be conquered, they call a vain promise. But in place of that they will be able to give you only ersatz liberations. The warning here is: "Do not let yourself be led astray. What they call 'the end of history' is not yet the end. So long as evil ruins the taste in the good deed, so long as the dead are dead, nothing is 'very good'; the end is not yet there." Therefore remain with Christ. Remain fools of the great world hope of God. "Let everything pass you by that passes itself off as already being fulfilled time. The world of death itself must be changed. . . . Until then the word of God has not yet happened" (Iwand). Do not have anything to do with fulfillments which bear the seed of resignation in themselves and lead you into melancholy.

Secondly: *do not let yourself be frightened.* That is the kernel of this warning. You will hear of wars and rumors of wars. Nation will rise up against nation and kingdom against kingdom. There will be famines and earthquakes. Everything that we love will be taken. There will no longer be anything firm in the political, social, indeed even the cosmic order. Trust will be for nothing. The foundations will shake.

We have experienced that; we do not need to paint a picture of it. But we also know how many then give up, despair, and in unceasing terror of a horror-stricken end wish for death. Only now is the comforting word supplied: it is not yet the end, but only the beginning of pain. What men consider as the end, because it grabs hold of everything where they live, is not yet the end. The world finds its end first in the return of Christ and the arrival of his kingdom. Premature despair is something we are not permitted. The end does not lie in the fear before which nothing on earth is certain; for not the catastrophe but the messianic kingdom of Jesus is the end. The Lord is not in wars, famines, and catastrophes. Therefore, let them pass by. Do not surrender to despair. Hold firmly on to hope. Nothing is yet lost.

Both warnings, "Do not let yourself be led astray" and "Do not let yourself be frightened," belong together. One is against itself trying to bring about the utopia of boldness, the end which is not yet there; the other, however, is against accepting the utopia of dark despair, misfortune, and catastrophe for the end, and not hoping for the kingdom of the death-awakening God. The hope for the future of Christ is the antidote against the presumptuous anticipation of heaven on earth, and against the despairing path of hell on earth. Both warnings sharpen the wakefulness of faith so that it remains in hope between illusion and resignation, between courage and despair.

In the second part of Jesus' speech, the terrors of history

and the future of the Christian church itself importune. From the fate and the future of the world, the emphasis turns to the fate and the future of the disciples of Jesus. The suffering spoken of here does not arise through outside circumstances but is first called forth through the life and witness of Christians. The suffering of persecution and the coldness of love actually corresponds here to the fateful suffering of the entire world. In this the Christian church becomes part of the continuing line and communion of the "sorrow of Israel."

"You will be hated by all nations for my name's sake." What Israel often experienced as a people of God in a godless world comes now to Christians. For with the gospel of the kingdom of all peoples they become a witness of hope, and, so far as they become that, they will also be laughed at as fools and hated as bringers of unrest. Evil itself will invade them: many will fall, be betrayed, and hate one another. The church offers no security either. It too is not yet the place of shelter, nor the end of history. The crisis of making judgments goes right through its people. False prophets will enter among them and lead them astray. By that, as the following sentences show, Matthew means the lawless ones. They do not like the fact that Jesus has not abolished the law but has instead fulfilled it with better righteousness. They fail to recognize that the love of faith must be a better righteousness on earth. If we think of a world court of justice, according to Matthew, where the coming world judge looks for deeds of love to the hungry, the captive, the thirsty, the forsaken, then can we say that this leading astray consists of lovelessness.

The unloving proclaim only a churchly Christ. They triumph religiously with the Resurrected but no longer hear him say: "What you have done to these the least of my brothers, you have done to me." They proclaim, thus, solidarity with the crucified Christ, with the Christ who waits on us in the hungry, the degraded, the forsaken. Therefore, love cools in many. We know that this coldness goes like a frost through our Western churches, and they harden into a clerical religious institution.

Thoughts of the future emerge again in the warning "He who endures to the end will be saved." There is salvation: it lies in persevering with Jesus until the end, until the kingdom of Christ. It lies in trust and remaining with Jesus and his word. Here in general is not intended the return from the evil world in the tranquility of the church or peace of heart. "Remaining and persevering" in this case means remaining and continuing in love. The world becomes cold and loveless. Men become lonely. No one knows anyone else. Mistrust lies like a fog over all human relations. Cold contempt undermines life. Cynical fatalism covers the battlefield of the unjust war. We know that on both small scale and large. If we are a thousandfold disappointed then everything is the same to us. If all good views are frustrated and sabotaged, then we give up and adjust ourselves or we run and howl with the wolves. That is darkness and gross coldness.

But whoever perseveres in hope remains in love. Because we hope in Christ, we do not let ourselves be embittered by all disappointments. We persevere in the love of Christ for the degraded and the wronged. We bring friendliness into a world of cold indifference. We are "fools" of love because we always give an advance of trust.

And then there is the other: "*This gospel of the kingdom will be preached throughout the whole world, as a testimony to all nations; and then the end will come.*" Perseverance until the end; that means going on ahead with the message of freedom and of the kingdom, penetrating to all places and circumstances with the conviction that the end is the kingdom of Christ. The only person who will remain until the end will be the one who, on God's account, does not stay where he is but goes on ahead; who goes to meet the coming God in the world. Christians do not have a point of view to defend, but a way they must travel and a front on which to battle the real suffering in the world that exists right now. At this front we should ignite with the gospel hope in an open, outgoing life and awaken faith in the haughty and the despised. On this front of sorrowing and oppressed creatures we must disseminate friendliness and love through their solidarity.

And—then the end of world need!

That is the last thing. Notice that it does not precede the descriptions of wars, catastrophes, and famines. It simply means that those things are not yet the end. Christian hope is no frightful expectation of catastrophes. Christ is not coming as "the great destroyer of all things" (Christoph Blumhardt), but here, where, in the dark history of hunger and war and earthquake, friendliness is disseminated, where the gospel of the kingdom is brought to all people for the witness of their hope. Here for the first time it is certain and definitive: "And then the end will come."

Christian hope is thus the hope of a love which takes the sorrow of humanity upon itself and looks for the kingdom where "peace and joy laugh." And Christ is coming as the judge who comforts all the deeply afflicted and raises the suffering to freedom.

The dark "end of the world" turns us in Christ to his recognizable loving and hopeful face. In the strifes of history, in its provisional fortune and misfortune, only two things are necessary because they actually turn the need around: (1) remain in love; bring friendliness into the world of darkness and cold indifference; (2) continue in spreading the gospel of the kingdom; bring to all men that witness of their hope. This love and this freedom are the signs of the return of Christ and of the end of the world in the midst of history. Do not let yourself be led astray. Do not let yourself be surprised. There are no other signs than the sign of Jesus: the love of him who died on the cross and the future of him who was awakened for your freedom, your life, your fortune. In this sign God will conquer over a lost world.

11

Joy in the Revolution of God

And Mary said,
"My soul magnifies the Lord,
and my spirit rejoices in God my Savior,
for he has regarded the low estate of his handmaiden.
For behold, henceforth all generations will call me blessed;
for he who is mighty has done great things for me,
and holy is his name.
And his mercy is on those who fear him
from generation to generation.
He has shown strength with his arm,
he has scattered the proud in the imagination of their hearts,
he has put down the mighty from their thrones,
and exalted those of low degree;
he has filled the hungry with good things,
and the rich he has sent empty away.
He has helped his servant Israel,
in remembrance of his mercy,
as he spoke to our fathers,
to Abraham and to his posterity for ever."

Luke 1:46–55, RSV

There have been few songs of joy since Schiller and Bee-thoven. No longer do we sing, "Joy, beautiful divine spark, daughter from Elysium," for anxiety and care lie nearer to us than the jubilation of the liberated. We know that joy is a very expensive, but also very vulnerable, gift. If our children hop with pleasure through the room, it warms our heart. We are really even a little envious because we can no longer rejoice and dance. Why not? We know too much!

Even the "joyous and blessed Christmastime" can easily lose its power to lift us out of the rut of the daily business grind and its vexations. That becomes truer than ever, more-over, in the face of suffering which goes now over the earth and cries without answer to heaven. Christmas in the warmth of our own homes may be a beautiful prospect for us, but for more than two-thirds of humanity there is no Christmas. There is not even enough to eat; there is no hope—only increasing sorrow. And that is not to speak of many continuing wars and international tensions. We know too much!

How can we feel so lightheartedly fortunate so long as men in Indochina are killed? How can we enjoy a traditional Christmas feast if, at the same time in India, children starve? How can we sing joyous songs if at the same time in other lands men are tortured? Do we not live in one world?! Must we not deny it, to be going around with a redeemed soul in this unredeemed world? Should we not be silent and wait, with those who are suffering, for a better future?

A joy which will truly grasp us in the face of the reality of our world should not have to be coaxed out of the distance, clothed in holiday dress, just to look at us with a Christmas face. For one cannot command himself or anyone else to soar to joy. Real joy must reach us in the depths where we ac-tually are. It must liberate us from the burden which actually weights us down. It must be a match for the power of evil and the despotism of suffering. It must show us and the oppressed of this world a future and bring the liberation in which everything shall become new. Otherwise joy remains waiting outside the door and does not enter. Otherwise it becomes an illusion which, to be sure, is beautiful, but swings powerlessly over our lives like a paper lantern. Otherwise Christmas would indeed become an island of the blessed beyond the circumstances in which others must suffer.

Out of Mary's song of praise sounds a note of joy in our life which we would otherwise not get to hear. It does not reach us from a height to which we cannot raise ourselves, but forces its way into the depths where we sit. It does not come in festive garments, but in the lowliness of a handmaiden. For it is the joy in a God who raises the lowly and satisfies the hungry, and fulfills his hopes in a forsaken people. If we hear this song of joy, however, we consider also all our own lamentations and the lamentations of the world which we read about daily in the newspapers. Let us recognize this God but not forget the burden which lies on us. Let us penetrate our world, in which so many are silent, with this joy in God. For then we will recognize the joy also, the irresistible joy of this God, which is deeper than irritation and trouble, and which possesses a longer breath than the evil in the world.

"My soul praises the Lord and my spirit rejoices in God, my Savior," says Mary. That cry goes through her with saving power. She forgets what most men say when they become rich. She does not say, "I am so happy: finally someone has thought of me also." No—her words "My soul praises the Lord" make him great who is great and does great things. It is as if she were to say, "I don't know who I am any longer or what I actually want." She is grasped by an unhoped-for love which makes all one's own wishes unimportant. Literally "beside herself" with joy, she forgets herself, forgets her hunger for life and her desire for fortune. That is more than just the breathing of a sigh of relief of a person who is free from need. It is the happiness of a person to whom the presence of God and the vision of his kingdom have become more important than one's own interests. Beyond that, it is in an individual way the fulfillment of a woman whose womb has been made literally the carrier of the savior of the world. The convulsion of self-fortune and the pain of self-reproach have fallen away from Mary. Her joy in God is without anxiety or pride. "My soul magnifies the Lord," she affirms.

Let us look still another minute at Mary herself, although she points so entirely away from herself. Who was she before this hour? A nobody or an everyman like us, a farmer's child out of Galilee, until God elects her and makes her into the mother of Christ. Not because she is pure and beautiful is she loved; but, on the contrary, because she is so loved and elected by God, she is pure and beautiful in her receptiveness. Who will she be after this hour? We know her path a little: the delivery outside in a stall in Bethlehem, and finally her tears under the martyr's fall of her son on Golgotha. But all this—her origin and the question, Who am I?; her future and the question, What will become of me and my child? are here forgotten. Whatever past started us off and whichever future may await us also—"My soul magnifies the Lord and my spirit rejoices in God."

Before she reflects as to whether it is love or suffering which has happened to her, she rejoices in God himself: that he is there now, that he comes and fulfills the hopes of forsaken man. Beyond good and evil, here is proclaimed a new era for the forsaken which will affect all men, and Mary has spontaneously seen that. God himself comes and breaks through the darkness which lies on earth and on every life: "But the Lord will arise upon you, and his glory will be seen upon" (Isa. 60:2). Here to an unknown maid from Galilee happens more than just the private relief of her need and a little luck for her. It is the turning point of all things that is proclaimed. The liberator from guilt, power, and oppression is born. Therefore, Mary rejoices entirely and wholly in God himself. Her joy is pure, for she does not want to use God in order to enjoy her life and her child. She gives her life out of hand and into the dawn of the new day of liberation.

Now what do we have left of our self-seeking questions "Where does that leave me? What is going to happen to me?" Only one thing remains here: "Strike through your ego and you are saved" (Luther), for God is coming and is already near you. We seek our fortune outside, carrying on our business and working hard to obtain it. God, however, is already there and in the midst of us in that child of Mary—in Jesus. And with him liberation and fortune, being loved and love are nearer to us than we know. Whoever recognizes that no longer needs to hunt that fortune nor try to become someone other than he is. He needs only to accept himself as he is because he is accepted by God how and wherever he is.

The joy of God which we hear in Mary's song of praise is full of peace and composure. No longer do we have to grit our teeth, but we can join in it, for it carries us beyond ourselves and into the current of freedom. Therefore, says Mary here with untroubled openness: "For he has seen the lowliness of his handmaiden." She is not ashamed of her insignificance. In her need for God, she does not have to place anything before others. Has not God seen her humbleness? Then she can rejoice also and extol her lowliness. In her blessed humility, children and the children of children, as the Scripture says, will praise her and not forget her for the sake of Christ.

How very much are we concerned, on the other hand, constantly to conquer our humbleness and to live on the sunny side of life, to show ourselves and others something. God, however, does not see the Pharisee or the Zealot, which we would gladly be, but the poor devil we are, whom we do not want to be at any cost. He does not take us seriously where we would like to be respectable, but frees us where we are somewhat pitiable. The joy in his liberation is deeper than the anxiety which is always constantly bound by our imaginations.

And in this liberation of God is the re-evaluation of all values of the inhuman. It is in Mary's song of praise, and it is dangerous. It is the song of a great revolution of hope, for this God in whom Mary so kindly rejoices moves the lowest to the highest. "He has shown strength with his arm, he has scattered the proud in the imagination of their hearts, he has put down the mighty from their thrones, and exalted those of low degree; he has filled the hungry with good things, and the rich he has sent empty away." That is in fact subversion and power. That sounds like the *Marseillaise* of the Christian front of liberation in the powerful battles and oppressions of this world.

There are other women in the Bible who sing such dangerous songs. At the exodus of Israel out of Egypt Miriam sang and beat on the drums: "Let us sing unto the Lord, for he has done a noble deed: horse and rider he has thrown into the sea." (Exod. 15:20–21). Thus sang Hanna: "The bows of the mighty are broken but the weak are girded about with strength" (1 Sam. 2:4). And here begins the history of Christ with Mary's song to the revolutionary God. "God" is no festival decoration for our holiday. God is a surpriser, but at the same time he is a noble God. "He leads into hell and out again." He calls his creation into life out of waste, wilderness, and darkness. He liberates the enslaved Israelites and casts the Egyptian slaveholders with their chariots and whips into the sea. He makes the troubled and complaining Job righteous, and he shames Job's pious friends. He leads Jesus, damned by the law and crucified by Roman power, out of death into his noble freedom. Where men do not want to be, where we often damn others, here this God comes and brings his lordship. Jesus, praising the blessed poor and lamenting the fate of the rich shows us the poor Lazarus in "Abraham's bosom" and the rich man in hell. Those who bear suffering he pronounces blessed, not those who lead others to suffering. Those who hunger after righteousness he makes into his confederates, not those who bend righteousness through power.

Whoever calls this God by name, whoever speaks of an "event which changes everything," speaks of a great revaluation of all values. With Christ we see a future dawn in which the powerful are overturned; the rich go out empty; and the proud, clever, and wise are dispersed. With Christ we see a future dawn in which the humble are raised and lift themselves and the hungry are filled with goods and rejoice.

Is this God partial? Does he not love all men without regard to persons? Yes, God wants everyone; but all as his people, as his image, as his free children. His nobility should reflect itself in everyone. All faces should be illumined in his clarity: evil, grimacing and crying faces, full and careworn faces. Therefore he lifts the degraded and insulted, the oppressed and burdened and the inhuman in his grace. And therefore he protests against the inhuman on the other side which destroys the life of others with power, riches, and selfishness. He disperses the haughty so that they become human out of their inhumanity. He pushes the mighty from their thrones so that they find again their humanity. He leaves the rich empty in order to win them for themselves and their neighbors.

The divine liberation of the poor and oppressed looks different from the liberation of the rich and the powerful. And with Jesus the justification of sinners looks different from the righteousness of the Pharisees. But the goal is the same: the conquering of that inhuman world in which not God but mammon, not love but anxiety, not freedom but law, not the Son of Man but power and fighting for riches reigns. It is not for revenge on the brutal that the oppressed are called out, but for their liberation from power. Not for lordship over the high are the humble lifted, but for the peace of God in brotherhood. Not for the enslavement of others is the slave freed, but for the abolition of slavery in general.

Paul once said in admirable clarity: "For consider your call, brethren; not many of you were wise according to worldly standards, not many were powerful, not many were of noble birth; but God chose what is foolish in the world to shame the wise, God chose what is weak in the world to shame the strong, God chose what is low and despised in the world, even things that are not, to bring to nothing things that are, so that no human being might boast in the presence of God. . . . Therefore, as it is written, 'Let him who boasts, boast of the Lord'" (1 Cor. 1:26–29;31).

It is the basis of all political revolutions (something we earlier recognized) that they, to be sure, free the oppressed but produce new oppression, because the oppressed cannot be liberated from the oppression in themselves. If, however, the oppressed are liberated so that they liberate the powerful from deeds of power, if the poor can be filled with goods in order to free the rich from greed; then the contradictions in this world will be saved, and the new man born who is neither oppressor or oppressed, but who in the unique lordship of God is entirely free.

The future of God is thus universal, shutting out no one, but including all as free men. But the way of God through this barbarous and inhuman world is concrete law and grace, disinheriting and exalting, fulfilling and making empty. For that God has, in the child of Mary, become man that he might make us from unfortunate and proud idols into true men. By his way to the cross he destroys the divinity which we perversely strive for, and recalls our humbleness which we despise.

That brings us to the last question—to the question of conscience: Do we rejoice over that? Actually rejoice if God comes to us as Mary said? On which side do we stand then?

Where do we find ourselves in the face of the Son of Man? Do we live with the Pharisees, the haughty, the powerful, and the rich? Or are we there somewhere between the sinners and the tax collectors, seeking those who bear suffering and those bearing righteousness, the poor, the guilty, the degraded?

Apparently it is not all the same. The freedom of God about which Mary rejoices in such a self-forgetful way encounters us in the man who was a friend of sinners and tax collectors, who died for the godless on the cross, who calls the poor, the captive, the naked, and hungering of this earth. In community with the Son of Man, Jesus, we find that unending, indestructible joy for and in the God of which Mary sings. We can hold it firmly, however, only in community with those who bear suffering and in solidarity with the captives. We live this joy when and wherever we partake in the liberating history of God who disperses and gathers, judges and frees, makes empty and satisfies—all that not out of anger and rage, but out of an overflowing joy in the freedom and in the peace of God. The first and the last word in the great liberation of God is joy, not hate; free speaking, not complaint. Out of the joy of God is Christ born, and in order to bring this contradictory world into joy he is killed and resurrected.

Let us go now into Christmastime not because it is like all the other years, but out of a unique joy for God and in God, and as a symbol of his future in a very unrecognizable, human-becoming world. Anxiety can infect, but joy still more; hate can break out, but freedom still more. To celebrate that is worthwhile and to disseminate it festively is good. If we have God, "the fact which changes everything," before our eyes, then we can also now and in the face of the unspeakable sorrow in the world, in our own country and hearts, sing: "My soul magnifies the Lord, and my spirit rejoices in God, my savior."

Dear Father in Heaven, we thank you that you yourself come, and with your joy in Jesus Christ are already in the midst of us. You did not despise the humbleness of your handmaiden, and you come with your spirit also in the secret corner of our poverty. We have nothing to offer to you other than the rags and tatters of the unknown. But you make us free and great. We rejoice in you in the name of Jesus. For the sake of your kingdom we bring now before you the cry of complaining creation. We ask you for peace; we ask you for freedom for the captives, for those persecuted for your sake, for the politically and racially oppressed; we pray to you.

We pray to you for your righteousness in the social conflicts and generational conflicts in our land.

We bring before you the sighs of the dumb and the bitterness of the hungry.

Lord, hear us. Complete your kingdom; reveal your power and nobility to all the forsaken and suffering creation. That we ask in the name of Jesus and for his sake.

12

Th∈ Basis for Hope in Life and Death

Hope for a human world

In a fairy tale which we all know from childhood, a young man sets out in order to learn the gruesome. Unfrightened, he has one adventure after another and finds nothing fearful. But then in the middle of the night he is doused by his wife with a bucket of cold water and little fish—nameless terror, a terror in which he no longer knows himself!

In real life, the story goes the other way: The young person does not set out in order to lose himself in frightful adventures but more often to find himself. He lives, but for what purpose he does not know. Though he works and enjoys, he may still not know what he actually wants. And, having lost himself, he would like to find himself again.

We always feel ourselves estranged from this life which forms and damages and disfigures us, which accompanies us out of hand without our wanting it. Each one of us who feels something of this alienation in his lived life, both personal and public, would like to set out to learn hope. We would like to set out and break out of our indiscernible, becoming life as soon as we grasp a tip of hope that it must actually be different and that it also could be different; that we do not have to stand over against ourselves and our neighbors in such an unrelated way; that the society in which we live does not have to be so cold and indifferent and inhuman; that this whole world does not yet have to bear "the darkness and the great coldness" but, on the contrary, that kingdom where peace and joy laugh.

Even in deep skepticism and with men who have resigned themselves to the failures of this life there burns at bottom the demand for true human existence and for a more human life. To be sure the great fervor with which men earlier, in the Enlightenment, broke out in revolutions and immigrations in order to find that other future is behind us. We know that not all budding dreams mature, that circumstances are more restrictive than youthful exuberance once thought. Even then, after many intelligent departures into the future, the soul of Europe is like a burnt-out crater landscape. We live, as it were, in the hardened lava of a cooled volcano. And we still know that to some extent and always in every case when we suffer in the frozen, immovable affairs of an alienated life somewhere.

Now it may be said that where others resigned themselves Christians always have hope and understand how to break away. On what do Christians hope? Let us gather the answers as we customarily encounter them on the world-denying side of Christian hope. Christians say: "We hope in God. We hope in the hereafter which will bring our suffering here on earth to an end. We hope for a life after death and for the return of the soul into its eternal home with God." Christians teach little children to pray with the words: "Dear God, make me good that I might enter into heaven."

An old Ascension hymn goes: "Draw us to thee;/Oh, grant that we/May walk the road to heaven!/Direct our way/Lest we should stray/And from thy paths be driven."

This Christian hope generally comes into print in funeral announcements and gives us the impression that Christian hope is good for dying but not for living, since it directs itself entirely to a better hereafter. We further obtain the impression that Christian hope penetrates only privately into our life here—in the soul, in the interior, in the heart and conscience. But we live bodily and suffer earthly; we are disappointed and wounded in our love for other men and we feel ourselves exhausted and alienated in our work. Shall the Christian hope comfort us only over the failures of this life? Does it not then rob us of exactly that power which we need for the responsibilities of this life, and for bringing something more friendly into this life? What help for us is a hope for an eternal home of the soul if we see others physically hungering and suffering?

When we are offered comfort of the soul and longing for the hereafter, this does not make hope strong, but weak. As the promised compensation of sorrow which we must suffer here, it makes us ready to be satisfied with ourselves, but not to change our circumstances. And still more: such a private hope for the hereafter actually makes men here loveless. We can pass by the suffering of this time for we know for ourselves something better. But as this hope directs the sense of man in an escapist way into a better hereafter, it leaves in the lurch the love which is necessary here.

In this world-denying side of Christian hope, we see clearly that hopes are ambiguous and can be misused. They can, as Karl Marx says, be the opium of the wishful dreams of a suffering people. They can, however, also be the protests of the degraded and offended against degradation and offense. Christian hope often operates in so opposite and so vainly promising a manner. Then it loses its orientation, no longer looking into the future but only above into heaven. Then it is the expression of a constant yearning for salvation from this world, but no longer a wonderful power for the changing of this world. Anyone who interprets Christian hope in this form knows only a neglected, decayed hope already devoured by resignation. It is time that Christians and non-Christians recognize again the original, world-changing side of Christian hope and experience: that Christianity is not only a religion of salvation, but at the same time an encompassing revolution of earthly affairs.

Christian faith is in its origin and in its essence a resurrection faith. What does that mean? It is the faith that out of his alienation and out of the deepest nonidentity with himself—death—man will come to himself, to his nature, and to his dignity in that future of God which has dawned with the resurrection of Jesus. Let me explain myself a little further.

When Jesus of Nazareth was here in his public ministry, he preached like John the Baptist: "The time is fulfilled, the kingdom of God is approaching. Repent and believe this word." John the Baptist, as his entrance fee into the coming kingdom of God and true human nature, had demanded repentance. Jesus, on the other hand, places no conditions: he heals the sick, speaks a word of freedom from oppression of guilt, eats with sinners and tax collectors. With him, repentance is not broken-heartedness, but joy in freedom, openness for the kingdom where peace and joy laugh. What men have held for the distant music of the future is present in his nearness.

From prison, John the Baptist sent his disciples to Jesus with the question: "Are you he who is to come, or shall we look for another?" Jesus answered: "Tell John what you have heard and seen: the blind see, the lame walk, the lepers are made pure, the deaf hear, the dead are resurrected, the poor have the kingdom preached to them. Blessed is he who does not find fault in me" (Matt. 11:2, 4–6). Thus, in the New Testament reports of the events of Jesus' coming we can see the fulfillment of age-old hopes. Our idea of the kingdom of God and of man in the kingdom as something for the hereafter, becomes, with Jesus, now, this time—the present, and entirely earthly. The future of that home for which our guilt and sorrow causes us to yearn so deeply, with Jesus forces itself into the present and becomes powerful in the present.

Now we know, however—and it is a daily experience—that this present did not remain. In his crucifixion, this nearness of God and of his kingdom disappeared. Jesus had helped others but could not help himself. His life, which was surrounded by the wonder of a fulfilled hope, ended without that wonder before the gates of Jerusalem in his crucifixion and in forsakenness by God. No one would have cared about him further. To everybody it was once again proven that this world *is* this world and the beyond is beyond. No one breaks through the walls if not just in this crucified one in whose Easter appearances those bitterly disappointed disciples had obtained the certainty of resurrection.

What does this mean? If resurrection of the dead has already taken place in Jesus, then can death no longer be the wall of separation between this side and that side. Then through him unconquerable life in the midst of death is already present. "In the midst of life we are surrounded by death" is provisional truth, but "In the midst of death we are encompassed by life" is then a full truth.

The barrier in which human hopes separate themselves, the transitoriness of fortune, and the death of love is already broken through in Christ. Even more firmly than in the miracle of healing, the hereafter has become the now in the resurrection of Jesus, for here the future of life in the presence of death is already apparent. Identity out of alienation, life out of death, home out of sorrow, the kingdom of God and of man against the enmity of death have become hopeful with that. Even more, the Christian hope in this event catches fire as it is born like the resurrection out of the Cross, out of disappointment, and out of godlessness. It becomes the hope of those who know the cross; in other words, it becomes the hope of those who know the rigors of godlessness and the abyss of the separation of God from the world.

No longer is this the hope of the religious, but of the poor. They come to hope where nothing more is to be hoped. It is a hope which overcomes its own disappointment and finds in its end its own beginning. It is not frivolous as many youthful hopes are, nor illusionary. It knows that its hope is first fulfilled when death is no more and the tears—here justified—are dried away. It directs itself thus not only to possibilities but also the hardest facts there are; and against death, because it reckons with the possibilities of God. It remains unsatisfied, pushing, protesting, and suffering in a world in which the suffering cry against Heaven.

The Christian hope of resurrection is not a hope for the hereafter or a life after death, but for a true human existence and the life of God against death. Hope for a life after death can be satisfied with death. In the New Testament, however, death is "the last enemy" of God and of man because in the resurrection of Christ a life has come near which has denied death.

Still, the old, world-denying side of the Christian hope has kept alive in all its misunderstanding the consciousness for man's severest alienation: guilt and death. If, however, Christian hope lives in that the hereafter of the kingdom, of the home, and identity in Jesus Christ has become this side, then it can and must direct itself here and now against the many small alienations and degradations of man.

Its world-changing side means love for man who has become a stranger to himself and to his neighbor, friendliness in a world of darkness and great cold, support for the poor and the suffering, for the degraded and the insulted.

And because the kingdom of God comes to earth, it is therefore valid to work here in a native earth. Because God's righteousness will dwell on earth, the battle for social righteousness is therefore also valid. Then on this earth on which the cross of Christ stood, righteousness and peace will kiss each other and happily praised will be those who establish peace and bring reconciliation. If the dying actually are called out of death into life, then life, work, and suffering succeed here in the light of a great promise. It becomes the anticipation, the encroachment, and the beginning of the true future of man. The Christian hope is loved in success and not in failure. It has basis for that in the unique and unforgettable event of the resurrection of Christ.

Hope against death

All hopes of man succeed sooner or later in their hardest test of verification—death. From the darkness in which man finds himself at the end, and which in the middle of his life is already spreading out from his impending death, just how much light his hope is able to cast becomes apparent. Man becomes aware of himself and his life because he knows about his death. His hopes originate at all times in the problem of death. Here they flicker, and here they collapse. There is no hope in death, if there is also no sustaining hope in life. But why is there something still to be hoped for in death? Is there a hope which also overcomes death?

From our Western intellectual history, we know two images of hope in the face of death: one is the Greek symbol of the immortality of the soul and the other is the biblical symbol of the resurrection of the dead. On the one side there is the certainty of the invulnerability of the soul in the death of the body, and on the other side the certainty that God will create new life out of death.

If asked which hope Christendom makes to the dying, Christians and atheists generally answer: hope for a life after death, hope for the immortal soul. The Christian confession of faith as stated in the worship service says: "I believe in the resurrection of the body and the life everlasting." And "I look for the resurrection of the dead and the life of the world to come."

How should we consider that?

The basic difference of both images of hope against death will become clear to us if we compare two kinds of dying with each other.

The Greek philosopher Plato depicted the death of Socrates for us in order to show what the immortality of the soul signifies and which deportment this recognition will confirm in death. Socrates, well-known as a godless man and seducer of youth, was sentenced to death by the poison cup. In his last hours he sat together with his students and exposited to them once again his philosophical insight and his deportment against death. Our body is only an external appearance which, so long as we live, hinders our soul's moving about freely and coming to itself, he said. Base passions and bodily pains bind it to this world where everything is unstable and fleeting and nothing true, lasting, and authentic is to be found. Thus the soul, our true self, is confined in the body as in a straitjacket. As in a prison, the soul lives here in the unknown and longs after its true home. The body, which is chained in the weal and woe of temporal things, is the grinding-house of the soul. Itself alienated here, it must constantly do things which do not belong to its true nature. Through insight and deliberation, however, the soul of man can already recognize here on earth its basis in eternity and its own unchanging nature and can thus obtain distance over against the fortune and pain of the world. What does death then mean for it?

Death makes the soul free from the body. It leads the soul out of the prison into the eternal home, out of temporality into immortality and out of a world of deception and appearance into eternal truth. Death can only eat that which is temporal and, therefore, belongs to the temporal. But if the soul is of immortal origin, then death cannot reach it. The most inner self of man is invulnerable and unassailable. Anyone who can find this insight, here, in life, is more than a match for death and can look forward to it in peace and contentment. The person who fears going into death only shows that his soul is still restricted in earthly passions and is not yet released and saved. But whoever has sensed the undying, unassailable kernel of his soul does not tremble when death cracks the corporal shell. He will greet death of the body as the friend of the soul.

When Socrates saw how one of his students who loved him suffered at the idea that he would soon lie as a corpse before him, he pointed out the surpassing irony. The true Socrates, at the moment of death, would already have escaped from the corpse over which the student would afterwards be grieving.

Here we have a "beautiful death" before us. Serene freedom and surpassing rest proceed from the dying Socrates.

Man dies entirely differently in the Old Testament. Let us listen here to the prayer of King Hezekiah in time of death:

> I said, In the noontide of my days
>   I must depart;
> I am consigned to the gates of Sheol
>   for the rest of my years.
> I said, I shall not see the Lord
>   in the land of the living;
> I shall look upon man no more
>   among the inhabitants of the world.
> My dwelling is plucked up and removed from me
>   like a shepherd's tent;
> like a weaver I have rolled up my life;
>   he cuts me off from the loom;
> from day to night thou dost bring me to an end;
> . . . .
> Like a swallow or a crane I clamor,
>   I moan like a dove.
> My eyes are weary with looking upward.

O Lord, I am oppressed; be thou my security!
....
For Sheol cannot thank thee,
    death cannot praise thee;
those who go down to the pit cannot hope
    for thy faithfulness.
The living, the living, he thanks thee,
    as I do this day;
the father makes known to the children
    thy faithfulness.

The Lord will save me.

(Isa. 38:10–12,14,18–20a, rsv)

Here before death, the king is anxious because he loves life. He cannot play about death in serene composure. Here death is so deadly because it completely annihilates man in body and soul, because it is godless and leads into God-forsakenness. It is a hell because one can no longer see and praise God there.

The death of Jesus is also not beautiful. Jesus begins "to tremble and to hesitate." His soul is grieved until death, and he prays that this cup will be taken from him. He dies with words of despair on his lips, "My God, my God, why hast thou forsaken me?" (Matt: 27:46, rsv). The fatalness of his death is the great forsakenness by God, by the spirit, by that inner support of eternity. Here death is no friend of the soul, but the enemy of man and the enemy of God. Therefore, Jesus dies "with loud cries and tears" as the letter to the Hebrews says (5:7, rsv), and not in self-possession and serene irony. In the face of this suffering death of Jesus on the cross, the disciples gained in his Easter appearances the assurance of his resurrection from the dead: Jesus, the first-born of the deceased, the originator of the resurrection of the dead. In him has "life out of death" appeared.

We understand now that this Christian hope for the resurrection by God is something other than the consciousness of the divine immortality of the soul. The hope of resurrection is a hope against death, for death is the "last enemy" of God and man. True life is a life in which death is conquered and annihilated; indeed, abolished. And we hope for such a life from God who showed his power in the resurrection of Jesus. Only when he also shows it to us will we sing:

> "Death is swallowed up in victory,"
> "O death, where is thy victory?
> O death where is thy sting?"

To God, who speaks to man in the resurrection of Christ, only a new world in which death is conquered and annihilated can be in accord. One must give way—either God or death. To anyone who holds death as final and unconquerable God will be dark. But whoever believes in God for the sake of Christ cannot hold death for the end. For the sake of God's divinity, he believes in the final victory of life, of the beloved and pledged life of promise. Therefore, he suffers here in death.

Now, we can conceive of the indestructible soul in the heaven of the spirit just as little as we can the eternal life of the resurrected from death. The mental image fails us because we must form our notions out of our experiences, and we have experienced neither of these. It is different also with hope than with our ideas. Faith and hope do not come out of experiences, but go before them. Faith does not come out of experience, but experience out of faith. We do not come out of experiences to faith, but out of faith to new experiences. We must ask therefore what shall go before us in faith and hope—the immortality of the soul or the hope of resurrection—and how we experience life and death in the one and the other.

The conviction of the unassailable immortality of the soul grounds itself always in a definite attitude towards life. It is the posture of distance and of dominance against fortune and suffering, against love and pain. The Greek philosophy of the life of stoicism reduced men to apathy, that is, to the loss of passions. Whether fortune or pain pass by in the world, it is nothing. Whoever binds himself to nothing, loves nothing too much, does not suffer either. Even-temperedness, indifference, and composure are the virtues of the wise person who, conscious of his origins out of another world, is therefore undisturbed by the conflicts of this world. But we must also see the positive aspects of this inner distance of man for the corporal world. Out of this distance are born authentic human characteristics: serenity, composure, the capacity to stay on top of things and not take oneself too seriously.

The hope for the resurrection from the dead establishes another life posture—the posture of love. In love man opens his heart. In it he binds his soul to the life of the beloved. In love, he does not want to protect himself and his soul. He forgets himself and gives himself. For love, life here is everything. This is what makes the death of the beloved so fatal. Suffering in this temporality catches hold of a soul which loves and privation makes it inconsolable. Its passion in the affair and in the beloved secures it this sorrow. Death then is not first known if man himself dies, but where the beloved dies, for we do not experience death in ourselves but in those we love.

How shall love overcome death without our delivering ourselves up and becoming indifferent? There must be a hope beyond death and against death in order for love to remain and for us not to resign. We need to understand the Christian hope of resurrection not simply as a distant speculation for circumstances after death. Only love, which gives itself wholly, here, sides with everything, binds itself passionately, grasps this hope, because this hope grasps it.

The hope of resurrection makes man ready to give up his life in love, to say yes totally to a life which is surrounded by death. The hope of resurrection makes us ready to take upon ourselves the pain and suffering which love brings. It does not withdraw our souls from this corporal, earthly life but inspires this earthly life with devotion, quick response, readiness of sacrifice, and joy. When, in love, we hope in such a way, we cast off the mantle of protection whereby a wounded heart can hide itself in indifference and irony. In love we give life out of hand into the expectation that God will awaken the dead and create new life out of the dust to which everything returns.

For this relationship of change of an outpouring love and hope of resurrection the Bible has used the image of the seed. "Truly, truly, I say to you, unless a grain of wheat falls into the earth and dies, it remains alone; but if it dies, it bears much fruit. He who loves his life loses it, and he who hates his life in this world will keep it for eternal life" (John 12:24–25, RSV). "You foolish man! What you sow does not come to life unless it dies" (1 Cor. 15:36, RSV). The hope of resurrection opens to love that future of God and that freedom needed for the ability to love. We experience here, then, in love, what the hope of resurrection actually is. And what love and the affirmation of life means in the mind of God is disclosed by the hope of resurrection.

With that we come to the last question: if the Christian hope of resurrection is separated so entirely from the conviction of the unchangeableness of the soul, is there then in this life which runs to death nothing that remains and endures and makes man invulnerable? Is the doctrine of the resurrection for the men of this life a sad truth? No, according to the Christian understanding, there is also already in this life something almost as indestructible which makes man secure from death. That is, for the apostle Paul, the spirit which moves out of the resurrection of Christ like a strong, irresistible wind through the life of the believing and the hoping. To be sure, they will also die. Body and soul, the whole man sinks into the grave. But, this spirit of resurrection confers to life an indestructible direction and openness to the future that reaches out over death into a life which overcomes death.

This spirit is not a substance in us, but a direction of our whole spiritual and corporal life. Wherever we give ourselves wholly to this direction, wherever we live entirely in the future of God, and draw the power of this future into our lives; there we overcome death, there we surpass, as it were, the coming death. Death comes too late. It meets us no longer. And that is no Utopia which flees into the hereafter, for this openness of man in the spirit of the hope of resurrection over death brings us into the life of love.

What it means—and more deeply, I think, than with Socrates—is clearly expressed in the first letter of John: "We know that we have passed out of death into life, because we love the brethren" (1 John 3:14, RSV).